Of Time and Place

The Fesler-Lampert *Minnesota Heritage Book* Series

This series is published with the generous assistance of
the John K. and Elsie Lampert Fesler Fund and David R. and
Elizabeth P. Fesler. Its mission is to republish significant
out-of-print books that contribute to our understanding and
appreciation of Minnesota and the Upper Midwest.

The Gift of the Deer by Helen Hoover

The Long-Shadowed Forest by Helen Hoover

North Star Country by Meridel Le Sueur

Listening Point by Sigurd F. Olson

The Lonely Land by Sigurd F. Olson

Of Time and Place by Sigurd F. Olson

Open Horizons by Sigurd F. Olson

Reflections from the North Country by Sigurd F. Olson

Runes of the North by Sigurd F. Olson

The Singing Wilderness by Sigurd F. Olson

Voyageur Country: The Story of Minnesota's National Park
by Robert Treuer

SIGURD F. OLSON

Of Time and Place

ILLUSTRATED BY LESLIE KOUBA

University of Minnesota Press

MINNEAPOLIS

First published in hardcover in the United States by Alfred A. Knopf, Inc.,
New York, and simultaneously in Canada by Random House of
Canada Limited, Toronto.
First University of Minnesota Press edition, 1998. Reprinted by
arrangement with Alfred A. Knopf, Inc.

Grateful acknowledgment is made for permission to reprint
previously published material:

"The Men Who Don't Fit In," by Robert Service, reprinted by permission
of Dodd, Mead & Company, Inc., from *The Collected Poems of Robert Service*,
copyright 1907, 1909, 1912 by Dodd, Mead & Company, Inc.; copyright 1940
by Robert Service; material from *The Collected Poems of Robert Service* also
reprinted by permission of McGraw-Hill Ryerson Limited. "The Old Canoe,"
by George T. Marsh, published in *Scribner's Magazine*, October 1908, copyright
1908 by Charles Scribner's Sons; copyright renewed; reprinted by permission
of Charles Scribner's Sons.

Published by the University of Minnesota Press
111 Third Avenue South, Suite 290
Minneapolis, MN 55401-2520
http://www.upress.umn.edu

Printed in the United States of America on acid-free paper

Library of Congress Cataloging-in-Publication Data
Olson, Sigurd F., 1899–1982
Of time and place / Sigurd F. Olson ; illustrated by Leslie Kouba.
p. cm. — (The Fesler-Lampert Minnesota heritage book series)
Originally published: New York : Knopf, 1982.
ISBN 0-8166-2995-1 (pbk. : alk. paper)
1. Natural history—United States. I. Title. II. Series.
QH104.O45 1998
508.73—dc21 98-21096

The University of Minnesota is an equal-opportunity
educator and employer.

10 09 08 07   10 9 8 7 6 5 4 3

To my family

Contents

Contents

Preface

The collection of experiences I have brought together in this book seems to fit into the broad pattern of what I have known in a lifetime of searching for meaning. Each experience is colored by my imagination and fantasy and grows out of an attachment to the land and a feeling for its antiquity. As I look back upon the many places I have been and upon the intimate relationships with natural things close to me, these vignettes are entwined in my thoughts and dreams.

No two individuals see the world in the same way. What has touched me may not affect you. But there is a common bond, for we are human, the only creatures on earth who can look at a scene with wonder and delight and sometimes with dismay. I have written about rocks, arrowheads, erratics, and mementos, things that have a very personal message for me. Some chapters tell of intangible things, mysterious and sacred things that have an emotional impact on our minds and spirits. And I also have talked about the great cycles of climatic change over which we have no control, the periods of drought, tornadoes, earthquakes, and glaciers. We simply accept them as inevitable, thankful we have survived, and have become convinced of the durability of the surface of the earth which we have been allowed to enjoy and love for a short time.

I offer this book to you in the hope you will find something of personal value, perhaps even a sense of recognition of some experiences in your own lives that resemble mine. Or perhaps it might be a guide to knowing; and if that turns out to be true, I shall be eternally grateful.

I wish to acknowledge the faith and encouragement of the members of my family, my wife, Elizabeth, Esther and Sigurd Jr., Yvonne and Robert. I especially wish to thank Ann Langen for the countless hours spent in editing the manuscript, also Angus Cameron, my esteemed editor, and his assistant, Barbara Bristol, who, in the book's final preparation, did everything possible to make *Of Time and Place* a distinctive and beautiful volume.

I value Thomas Gray's "Elegy Written in a Country Churchyard," Sidney Lanier's "The Marshes of Glynn," William Cullen Bryant's lovely poem "To a Waterfowl," Robert W. Service's "The Men That Don't Fit In," and Henry Wadsworth Longfellow's moving stanzas from "Evangeline" beginning "This is the forest primeval."

Of Time and Place

Of Time and Place

Over the years the voyageurs, as we called ourselves, made many trips together retracing routes of the old voyageurs in their far-flung travels along the rivers and lakes during the days of the fur trade. No matter where we decided to go it was a joyous adventure, for we were one with them and with the explorers who mapped the far Northwest for the first time.

We ran the same rapids, knew the waves on the same big lakes, and suffered the same privations. Though ours was a modern age, we knew the winds still blew as they had then; the dim horizons looming out of the distance were no different from the mirages they had known. In the mornings we saw the same mists, resembling white horses galloping out of the bays. We knew all this, but most important was the deep companionship we found together. We had been most everywhere, and for us the North was much more than just terrain. We were part of its history.

Like men who had been in combat, we looked at the world

3

through different eyes, for we had been tested in the crucible
of wilderness travel and had not failed. The values we shared
from our common experience are hard to explain, but without
them life has no purpose. In my homeland of the Quetico-
Superior and the wilderness canoe country, I often think of
these values, which are in the land itself and in its rich history.
The real importance of this region I know so well is not the
vast deposits of minerals and timber or the part they play in
our economy; the real importance lies in the values we find
there and that we take with us when we leave, although we
may not quite understand them.

I am always eager to renew old associations from my voyageur days. On one occasion I spent a few days with my old
friend Tony Lovink. We headed west from the city of Ottawa
and made a foray into the Gatineau country of southwestern
Quebec, climbing to the very crest of the great escarpment.

It was autumn and the forests were gaudy with color. After
a long steep ascent, we reached a bare ledge bathed in sunshine
where we ate our lunch and rested on a grassy place, looking
up at three ravens wheeling and soaring in the blue sky. Far
below lay the fertile Ottawa Valley, broad and lush, the river
winding its way west before it turned north to Lake Nipissing,
then south to Georgian Bay and the beginning of the Great
Lakes. Beyond was the misty horizon of the Laurentian divide,
where the rivers run north to Ungava Bay of Quebec and
Labrador.

I thought of the war between the French and the British in
1759 when General James Wolfe laid siege to the impregnable
fortress of the city of Quebec. When the time came to storm
the battlements, the British were faced on the Plains of
Abraham by the brilliant Marquis de Montcalm. It was then
that Wolfe's "thin red line" was broken and both generals

received grievous and fatal wounds. That day Quebec fell to British arms, and France's dreams of an inland empire in the New World were swept away.

As General Wolfe lay dying, he is supposed to have said, "I would rather have written Gray's 'Elegy Written in a Country Churchyard' than taken Quebec." I, too, sometimes think what really counts are the songs and poems men write to sum up the terrible experience of war. Thomas Gray said it all too well in his famous elegy:

> The boast of heraldry, the pomp of pow'r,
> And all that beauty, all that wealth e'er gave,
> Awaits alike the inevitable hour:
> The paths of glory lead but to the grave.

There are many beautiful poems, all evoking images, each symbolizing how we feel about the places we have known. One image treasured over the years is from William Cullen Bryant's "To a Waterfowl":

> Whither, midst falling dew,
> While glow the heavens with the last steps of day,
> Far, through their rosy depths, dost thou pursue
> Thy solitary way?

This does something to me, perhaps because in my youth I was a duck hunter. It evokes sunsets on the marshes, the whisper of wings overhead, long wavering skeins of ducks against the blaze of the sky. No one can ever know what this really means unless he has lived with the scene Bryant captured.

One day toward the close of the Second World War, I walked along a river in Germany. It was quiet at dusk with a dull glow in the west. On both sides were silhouettes of bombed buildings, and a bridge lay broken in two in the current. It was spring and I was far from home, and then, as though out of the past, I heard a familiar sound, the whistle of wings overhead. I looked up and saw a flight of mallards heading down the river. For a moment I forgot everything and was back in the rice beds of the Minnesota lakes.

Once on a pack trip in the Sun River country of Montana, we were riding through a dense stand of spruce in the bottom of a canyon. I got off my horse to lead it around a windfall, and in the center of the trail in a muddy spot was the distinct imprint of a huge grizzly. We never saw the bear, though we found deep gashes he had made in the bark of a spruce as high as he could reach. From that moment the country was changed for me: it was the land of the mountain men of another century, that of Lewis and Clark and of the West.

John Muir said the Sequoias belonged to the solitudes and the millennia. I was in the Sequoias long after Muir had been there, and as I looked up through the great trees I felt as he did, that it was a moving experience. To realize they were mature long before the continent was discovered, and their lives reached back to the beginnings of Western civilization, was sobering to a short-lived man and his ambitions.

All such things belong to the world of place and time; they have been engraved in our memories, cherished moments that seem dearer than life itself. It is easiest for me to think of such moments in the Quetico-Superior or the Far North, for they have meant much to all voyageurs—the vistas, the solitudes, and the enormous quiet that have been around us everywhere.

While voyageurs no longer embark on long and hazardous expeditions into the bush, they have not forgotten and never will, so I shall end this essay on time and place with a poem

Of Time and Place

by George Marsh written at the turn of the century, long before we moderns traversed the hinterlands. Because we were familiar with the land he wrote about and traveled the same country, I know my old friends would understand the poem's meaning and the pathos that runs through it.

THE OLD CANOE

My seams gape wide so I'm tossed aside
To rot on a lonely shore
While the leaves and mould like a shroud enfold,
For the last of my trails are o'er;
But I float in dreams on Northland streams
That never again I'll see,
As I lie on the marge of the old portage
With grief for company.

When the sunset gilds the timbered hills
That guard Timagami,
And the moonbeams play on far James Bay
By the brink of the frozen sea,
In phantom guise my Spirit flies
As the dream blades dip and swing
Where the waters flow from the Long Ago
In the spell of the beck'ning spring.

Do the cow-moose call on the Montreal
When the first frost bites the air,
And the mists unfold from the red and gold
That the autumn ridges wear?
When the white falls roar as they did of yore
On the Lady Evelyn,
Do the square-tail leap from the black pools deep
Where the pictured rocks begin?

7

Oh! the fur-fleets sing on Timiskaming
As the ashen paddles bend,
And the crews carouse at Rupert House
At the sullen winter's end;
But my days are done where the lean wolves run,
And I ripple no more the path
Where the gray geese race 'cross the red moon's face
From the white wind's Arctic wrath.

Tho' the death fraught way from the Saguenay
To the storied Nipigon
Once knew me well, now a crumbling shell
I watch the years roll on,
While in memory's haze I live the days
That forever are gone from me,
As I rot on the marge of the old portage
With grief for company.

Scribner's Magazine, October 1908

The Sturgeon

All over the North we find the name Sturgeon, for early in the region's history the fish was common: some places are the Sturgeon Weir on the Churchill River in Canada, where the Indians set traps for them, Sturgeon Lake about sixty miles south of my home in Ely, Minnesota, and Sturgeon Bay on Lake Michigan.

The sturgeon is a primitive fish that feeds on the bottom, taking up whatever food it can find with a suckerlike mouth. It is sometimes caught in great nets set for other fish or speared below rapids, but usually it is baited with a ball of dough or a bit of putrid meat. When I was a boy living near a little fishing village on the Door County Peninsula of Wisconsin I saw a huge one. The lucky fisherman guessed it weighed four hundred pounds or more and was very proud of his catch.

Because of pollution in some areas the sturgeon has declined. Happily it is coming back as the rivers and lakes are cleaned of seepage, oil spills, garbage, and chemical wastes. It is heartening to note that even the Hudson River in New York now produces sturgeon of considerable size. In the Caspian Sea and the Black Sea in Russia, where sturgeon is famous for its black and golden roe and exquisitely smoked meat, pollution problems are also being controlled and the catch severely restricted.

As a guide in the Quetico-Superior country years ago, I watched the Indians spear them from a platform built over the foaming rapids of the Snake River below their village. Joe Moose, an old friend of mine, loved to spear them and always had a few at his little cabin. I stopped each time I went that way and would exchange bacon, flour, salt, or whatever he was short of for a sturgeon. Once I traded for one weighing about six pounds, a beautiful fish nicely smoked, brown and flavorful. I did not want a larger one because it would be hard to carry on my travels. This one was about three feet long, well shaped and firm. What a feast it would be during the days ahead, especially for snacks at noon or even while paddling.

After I had chosen my fish from the smoking rack and placed it against the cabin, I went inside to have a cup of tea and some bannock I'd brought along. This was always a ritual with Joe, for it consummated a bargain just like a factor at the trading post, sealing the deal with a drink of rum.

We visited about the weather, the presence of moose, deer, and wolves, and how the trapping had gone the winter before, which old Indians had passed away since my last visit. At last it was time to go and I picked up my gear and stepped out the door. Where was my sturgeon? It was gone. I looked everywhere, thinking it had fallen off the little porch, but it was nowhere to be seen. My anticipated joy of nibbling on a sliver of smoked meat vanished.

Joe Moose watched impassively while the search went on. "Where is it?" I asked with some irritation.

"Dog, she got him, always big tief. I'll whip him when she's come home," he assured me.

"But I paid you for the sturgeon," I insisted. "You'll have to give me another."

"You should have bring him inside," he said, "you should have know better. White man always foolish."

So it has been and always will be. The fabric of one's life is woven of varied experiences, some good, some bad, others just laced with humor.

Golden Trout

"Until a man has taken a golden trout and seen the Kern Plateau, he has not lived," Ardis Walker once told me. I had never forgotten, and one October several years later, I decided to find out if what he said was true. Ardis is no ordinary fisherman and going with him was no everyday adventure. Descended from that famous old mountain man Joe Walker, after whom Walker Pass through the southern Sierras is named, Ardis is a mountain man who loves this country more than any other place on earth.

He has the soul of a poet, is an artist with the dry fly, and is convinced that taking a golden is just about as far as a man can go in aesthetic experience. Like most who have put wet flies and garden hackles behind them for a light outfit and gossamer leaders, he had entered that rarefied atmosphere in which the actual landing of a trout is not as important as what happens to the fisherman's mind and character.

"What's more," he told me, "the country is as much a part

of fishing as the golden trout themselves. A man must become one with the terrain, the big old trees of the plateau, the golden color of the sand in the creeks, grassy meadows, and little canyons of which it is a part. Going into that country and getting the feel of it is important, and without it, no one can understand what these trout mean."

All this was my dream as I approached our rendezvous and the plane droned on into the night on its way to Los Angeles. The order "Fasten your seat belts" roused me from my reverie and I looked out the window at the great city, a sprawling tapestry of misty colored lights reaching endlessly into the dark. I would soon meet Ardis and go with him into the mountains two hundred miles to the north.

I studied the map he had sent me. Just below Mount Whitney, flanked by ranges of mountains on one side and the Mojave Desert on the other, was the Kern Plateau cradled by the two forks of the Kern River. It was wilderness country without roads or settlements, pinpoints of light, or anything to mar its beauty. "So rare and significant is the Kern Plateau with its clean water, pure air, and vistas of distance, nothing," said Ardis, "must ever be allowed to change it, for through some miracle this land has lain virgin and untouched since the day of the Spanish conquistadors."

When we landed the smog was heavy and in the probing headlights and neon signs was a sense of unreality, tremendous crowding, a vast confusion of sounds, smells, and vibrations a world away from the thoughts of wild country and golden trout.

The following morning I drove north through the desert, then northeast up a tortuous mountain road paralleling the Kern River which drains the plateau, and arrived at last at the little resort and lumbering town where Ardis lived.

He had not changed, the weather-beaten face, the deep wrinkles at the corners of his eyes, the Stetson, riding boots, and old leather jacket. A small plane was waiting on a strip nearby.

"Figured as long as you've only a few days to spend up here, you might as well take a look at the whole layout before we ride in," he said.

Within minutes we were soaring over a gently sloping tableland between the ranges. There were scattered stands of timber on a series of almost level parkland benches, the whole interlaced with meandering streams trickling through green grassy meadows.

"Golden trout country," said Ardis, "nothing like it in the whole West. That plateau is a museum piece, a geological accident. Missed by the continental glaciers, it is thus raised and tilted. The trout were trapped on top and have lived there for thousands of years. It's an ecological island and like most is fragile and delicate. Cut the trees, disturb the soil, or change it in any way and the trout would disappear."

Ardis could not talk this way if he did not know the score, for in his youth in the eastern part of the U.S. he had been an engineer, well educated in the sciences, and had left it all to come back to the mountains to live. The blood of old Joe Walker could not be denied.

We skirted the barren slopes of Mount Whitney, turned, and flew down the deep canyons of the north fork of the Kern with its brawling rapids and foam-flecked pools. As we swung over the timber and meadow country, he pointed out the land along the southern edge, the rounded granitic formations gleaming in the sun.

"The goldens," he told me, "come only from the drainage basin of the south fork; mostly rainbows in the north."

We turned and headed for town and in a few moments were on the runway. I threw my gear into a Land Rover and we drove north along the river about twenty miles, then turned off and for another eight miles followed an old logging road leading to the pack station, where we would get our horses and outfits.

It was a pleasure watching the wranglers load the pack string. Mountain men, desert men, canoe men, they are the same the world over—only the land differs. They move easily and the difficult job of getting any outfit under way is accomplished with no apparent strain or effort. The country has done something to these men, given them calmness and imperturbability, the mark of the wilderness.

It was good to get on a horse again, to feel the surefooted progress up a mountain trail. As we climbed to timberline, we left the sage and rabbit brush, the piñon pine and scrub oak, and began to see big trees, Jeffrey and white pine, fir and lodgepole. Patches of the rosy brown stems of mountain mahogany showed in the sparse undercover as well as a few late-blooming flowers. To my delight I found a cluster of Indian paintbrush flaming against the side of the trail.

As we topped the pass, we looked to the north over a sweep of scraggly, wind-tortured pine and fir whose frayed and ragged tops leaned away from the prevailing gales. Far beyond was Mount Whitney, brooding as always over the plateau. Unchanged from when the mountain men came through, this is still a land of silences, ancient trees, and far vistas. It was unbelievable that within an easy day's drive lived millions of people.

The trail led from one level bench to another, and from each the vistas were the same—across the distance, colonnades of trees. That night in camp beside a dying fire we watched the moon silvering huge boles of the trees. An owl hooted and from nearby came the soft music of running water. Los Angeles, its smog and roaring traffic, seemed far away. This was the country old Joe Walker knew a century ago.

In the morning we rode toward the valley of Trout Creek, one of the many little streams meandering through a network of meadows, and finally burst through a fringing grove of lodgepole. Dismounting, we tied our horses and approached stealthily.

"They scare easily," whispered Ardis, "so no tromping around or talking." I quickly saw the reason why: the water was crystal clear and a few inches deep. Ardis fitted out his fly rod and started to cast. I had not come to fish, but to watch a master at his work.

In a few moments, flicking a tiny Royal over a riffle and just below a rock, he caught his first trout, the back mottled bronze and gold, a broad rainbow stripe extending onto the gill covers, belly aflame, rosy fins tipped with white—the scientific name, *Salmo agua-bonite,* the golden trout of the Sierras.

I knelt beside the bank and studied the bottom sand and gravel; the stones were golden too, the water over them the reflection of molten metal. After years trapped on their island plateau, they had become adapted to their environment.

I waited until Ardis was far enough away so any movement of mine would not frighten the fish and followed along quietly, watching his every move as he worked his way cautiously upstream. He was taking trout steadily from underneath smooth grassy banks, behind shallow riffles barely deep enough to cover them. Though he did not keep any of them, I knew the artistry and joy involved. In one shallow place the trout seemed to come out sideways to take the fly, and if they missed they'd go back the same way. It all went so swiftly I could barely tell what was going on.

I laid his last catch on a clump of blue gentian and admired the contrast of blue and gold against a background of green. We left the meadows and worked our way down a little roaring canyon where cliffs crowded closely. The stream churned its way over rocks and in between them, emerging for a moment only to be lost against the broken talus of the creek bed. There was a tiny waterfall, and the pool below was splattered with gold and silver droplets. This was a challenge I knew could only be approached from behind. For a while Ardis studied the situation, then crept as close as he dared.

He cast and the fly hovered over the spray, just far enough so it wouldn't get wet. A dip of the rod tip and it looked like the tiny gnat was fighting desperately to keep from being engulfed; I had never seen that dance of death done with such finesse. Then came the flash of gold all but exploding out of the spray, a wild dashing about the pool, and a swift scoop of the net.

Ardis laughed. "This is a real beauty," he said; "I'll bring it over." And he scrambled over the rocks to my hiding place. I took the fish out of the net, turned it over again and again, held it up against the sky, and marveled at it.

There were many such little falls and cataracts, each with its own particular problem, but one always solved with the coordination only an artist knows. The trout, seldom over eight or nine inches in length, could grow no larger in such little waters, but they made up for lack of size with beauty and dash.

"There are nearly two hundred miles of these creeks winding through the plateau," Ardis told me. "A man can spend two weeks in here fishing a different trickle each day."

When it was time to return, we packed and moved out through the timber. I had seen the golden trout, savored the country that produced them, and discovered what Ardis meant when he said one must get the feel of the land itself in order to appreciate them.

As we rode on I learned of a plan of land management that called for logging the timber and building roads and campsites that would destroy the wilderness quality of the Kern Plateau. I looked around at the timber, not of great value, and down into a deep valley where an unseen creek rippled over golden stones and the only sounds were those of soft ruffling on the water and of wind in the big pines. It was then Ardis told me about his long battle to stop the cutting of trees, such an integral part of the country we had seen.

"This fragile area," he told me, "should be thought of as a work of art, a masterpiece perfected through the long processes of geological and ecological evolution. Because of its rarity and beauty, we should approach it with reverence, gentleness, and restraint, knowing how swiftly it could tarnish."

Ardis continued: "The plateau of the golden trout with its little streams, grassy meadows, and tiny boiling canyons should be preserved forever and its great old trees kept as cathedrals of the spirit. To do otherwise is to disregard its real value. The region has a vital role to play, one involved with intangible values and dreams of mankind. Here is part of America as it used to be."

We should preserve our silent sanctuaries, for in them we perpetuate the eternal perspectives.

Ancient Trails

Mankind, in its eternal quest for food, treasure, and living space, has left a crisscross of trails over the continents. Many of these trails are centuries old, and some go back thousands of years, further than any written historical record. They have always intrigued me; I have followed those I know, and as I traveled over them I felt a part of yesterday. These ancient traces of past migrations have great significance in any concept of time and place for they have affected our civilization and more importantly, perhaps, our minds and attitudes. Entire cultures were shaped by what trailblazers found on their forays into the vast unknowns of the early world.

Once I retraced Daniel Boone's trail through Cumberland Gap, made by this indomitable explorer as he felt his way toward the dark and bloody ground of Kentucky. Knowing as he did that he had to face hostile Indians and daily uncertainties, he considered himself fortunate to survive. What drove him on was both the fact that he was opening the door for settlers who were waiting to hear what he had learned and the sense of ultimate destiny and new lands to conquer. Though captured by Indians time and again, he always escaped. Boone was a fabulous woodsman, and nothing seemed to deter him. As I gazed over the land ahead with its tremendous hazards, trying to relive the first time he saw it, I could spot no sign of civilization; only forested hills and valleys lay before me, as they had been long ago.

Boone was typical of all mountain men of the West: he could not sleep if there were beaver to trap, or a grand summer rendezvous to look forward to where they could trade their furs, carouse, and gamble until all their wealth was gone. It wasn't the money that attracted them, but the life of freedom and danger. The chances of ambush and torture, death by arrows or tomahawks, were part of the game they played and the price was not too high. Few of them left the mountains, but died there as was their wish.

I think of the trails across the burning deserts: the Santa Fe, the Choohauhua; the trail to Mexico, Sonora, Guadalupe; the Coronado and the Oregon. As I think of these fading remnants of a bygone age I feel the unceasing desire all men have in the eternal quest.

I know well the water trails of the voyageurs and early explorers, for I have followed many by canoe; they, too, mapped the country for those to come. I have traveled their routes in the Quetico-Superior and in the far reaches of Canada's Northwest Territories, the Yukon, and Alaska. The voyageurs took dangerous rapids and violent storms in their stride on the Great Lakes, Lake Athabasca, Great Slave Lake, Great Bear Lake, and the rivers running into Hudson Bay. Nothing seemed impossible to this breed of men, who loved the life they had found. Starting at Montreal they worked their way down the border and from Grand Portage post on Lake Superior fanned out to the north, and into the Far West and Southwest. They left their trails everywhere for all to see, marked by names such as Lac la Croix, Grand Marais, Maligne, and Fond du Lac. The voyageurs suffered as all men do when they move into lands they have never seen before, and they epitomize in their own way what has motivated all adventurers since the beginning of time. The land they explored had a certain genius of its own but was marked forever by their passing. Those who are fortunate enough to pursue any of these trails become part of the ancient dream.

On the North American continent the frontiers seem very close, and we can almost hear the songs of voyageurs and the rumble of caravans heading west. When I look back I am glad the old trails have branded me too, as the maverick we all are. It is good to know there is an escape if we choose to take it, for there are still many wild and beautiful places as primitive as ever. The mountains, deserts, plains, and wild roaring rapids are waiting for you.

Great adventures beckon to all of us. We don't know where they will take us or if we will return, but for one brief moment in history we can be Daniel Boones, mountain men, or great voyageurs. The stakes may be high, but we accept them.

Mementos

In my cabin I am surrounded by many mementos, each bringing to life an old experience. Hanging in one corner are a couple of blackened tin pails from a canoe trip down the Hayes River, which empties into Hudson Bay. How well I remember the rapids we ran there and how we lost all of our cooking outfit and much of our food. In the larger pail are two wooden spoons—the only utensils recovered. Somehow all six of us survived without food in the bitter cold for the next two weeks. As I look back, the situation does not seem as desperate any more, for I can laugh at the good things and remember the comradeship of my fellow voyageurs.

Above the fireplace is a twenty-four-inch skin boat given to us by an Indian chief at Fort Franklin, on the western shore of Great Bear Lake. He asked me to place it in my cabin two thousand miles away and to think of him and his tribe each time we looked at it. The boat is carefully made of caribou hide, for there were no birch trees in that country, and even the paddles are authentic.

On the wall is a set of caribou horn tips I found at an Indian cabin not far from where we lost our outfit on the Hayes. At first, I thought it was a baby rattle, for when I moved it slightly by shaking the brown leather thongs which held it together, it made an odd, clicking noise. But as I studied it, I realized that it was a decoy made to attract caribou. An Indian told me later it was used by hunters long before the white man came. As caribou migrate over the rocks and tundra, their ankle bones make a clicking sound. Hunters, lying in wait behind a tussock of grass or willow, would rattle the decoys, and the caribou, always curious, would move toward the sound expecting to find others of their band. When the animals were close, the Indians would hurl a spear or shoot them with arrows.

On a nail is a pair of leather gloves and moccasins given me by Father Moraud, who served the Crees on the Churchill River. They are beautifully made and the bead design is one Indian women have used since the days of the fur trade several centuries back. When I hold them I think of life in the Far North, and of Father Moraud's devotion to his work. They are more than a gift; they are part of another time.

Hanging over the mantel is a pair of old Finnish skis which I used in my early days. Made in Helsinki, seven and one half feet long with leather toe straps, they served me well as I traveled many miles on them over frozen lakes. Near them is a weathered gray sign I came across on the Island River not far from my home. It had been nailed to a tree blown down where a small bridge once crossed the stream. The trail had been abandoned long ago, but the sign read:

10 MILES TO THE ISABELLA CABIN
2 MILES TO BOG CREEK TRAIL

Another cherished memento are two pairs of small exquisitely made Chippewa snowshoes, which remind me of Big Annie, a Chippewa woman. Years ago while teaching biology at the local college, during the Christmas holiday season I would snowshoe to Basswood Lake fifteen miles away carrying a packsack of presents for Annie's numerous brood. The children looked forward to my annual visits, and I was always greeted with cries of delight.

One unforgettable morning in the spring Big Annie came down on one of the boats to Winton, Minnesota, where I had planned to meet her. In her arms was a huge bundle carefully wrapped in an old canvas tarpaulin, which she gave me. I peeled off the outside and to my surprise found four pairs of snowshoes, a large pair for me, four feet long, a shorter one of three feet for my wife, Elizabeth, and two very small ones for our two boys.

"Why all this?" I asked her. "Whom are they for?" She grinned and then blurted out, "They for you, for the Bug Santa Claus. You teach bugs, don't you?" I nodded in bewildered pleasure as the truth finally dawned that she was alluding to my biology classes. We still refer to the two pairs of tiny snowshoes as belonging to the Bug Santa Claus.

Two ash paddles hang on a wall, one very weathered, the other new and beautifully shaped. On a far northern trip I broke my favorite paddle in a rapids, a desperate situation for the paddle was irretrievable. I could, of course, have whittled one out of a piece of split cedar, but it would never have been the same. When we reached a Hudson Bay post, I asked the factor if he had a good paddle I could buy. He shook his head and then brightened, went into his storeroom, and came out with a beauty, his own personal blade. "You can have it," he said, and would accept nothing. This was a paddle any voya-

geur would cherish and guard, and I accepted it with gratitude and humility at such a generous gesture. The new paddle is one a friend made of ash selected by him in a swamp where the trees grow straight and the fibers true. Now it hangs rubbed and polished with oil and wax until it gleams.

Paddles were important to canoe men during the early voyageur days, and one was often passed on from father to son, just as a sash was handed down. This will belong to my elder son and I know he will treasure it as I have.

Mementos have a strange power of evoking memories, but more than that they are a part of time and place.

The Marshes
of Glynn

A land can be colored by a poem or some particular utterance
that catches the mood and spirit of a place, as when I first saw
the Marshes of Glynn, so beautifully described by Sidney
Lanier in his poem of the same title. During my boyhood I
treasured his poems, learned to love them for their sense of
wonder and mystery, but it was not until I participated in a
survey of Cumberland Island, one of the famous Sea Islands
off the southern coast of Georgia, that I really appreciated
what he had written. We passed the Marshes of Glynn one day
on our way to the island and when I stopped there to read his
poem, I understood what he really meant.

> And now from the Vast of the Lord will the waters of
>   sleep
> Roll in on the souls of men,
> But who will reveal to our waking ken
> The forms that swim and the shapes that creep
>   Under the waters of sleep?

28

And I would I could know what swimmeth below when
    the tide comes in
On the length and the breadth of the marvellous Marshes
    of Glynn.

The poem set the tone for all that was to come on that survey. For me it was part of Cumberland and its exotic beauty: twenty-six miles of unchanged sandy beach, the screaming gulls and seabirds, the great sand dunes above them and beyond sight. Hidden in the jungles of a bygone age of our history, the island was within a stone's throw of the civilized southeast coast. Miraculously it had escaped the devastation of modern development and lay there in the sunshine as the sailors of the Spanish galleons had seen it hundreds of years before when they waded ashore through the surf.

There was an old roadway beyond those dunes almost all the way along the island. Obscured by the lushness of tropical growth there were old mansions crumbling into decay and mold, with hanging mosses and vines festooning them, some creeping through doors and windows. We went into the largest and found embedded in the broad mantel of the fireplace a plaque reading:

This is our sacred hearth
Here our eternal flame.

Feeling like intruders, we tiptoed around without speaking, until one of our crew whispered, "These mansions according to Park Service records were built by the Carnegie family during the last part of the nineteenth century."

We could imagine gay parties there when the wealthy came from all corners of the earth. On the table in the center of the room was a register of guests who represented a world of power and influence. I tried to picture the men in formal black and white, the long dresses, the old formalities, the gleam of silver and glassware, the carefree banter and frivolity. Someone had felt more deeply: "This is our sacred hearth . . ."

I decided to come back and see it by moonlight as Sidney Lanier would have done. I wondered what poem might have come from his visit, for he would have captured it all as he had in "The Marshes of Glynn." The night I was there the mansion was flooded with light. An old door creaked as it swung on rusty hinges in the soft night breeze and bats flew in and out. It was an eerie, ghostly place of "ghoulies . . . and beasties / And things that go bump in the night," a haunted place if ever I saw one! I did not stay long but took the trail back to the beach and away from the gloom. The moon made a broad path of light on the ocean and a few seabirds screamed as I disturbed them; then I heard only the slow wash of the waves.

The next morning I returned and walked the beach. The feeling of the night before was gone, for the day was sparkling and bright and birds wheeled and called as when I had first come. I looked at the dunes and along the high rim saw a row of curious burros, descendants of those the Spaniards had brought with them in the 1500's. I walked the length of the beach, and there was no sign of occupancy and use except at the broken pier at the far southern end. The storms of the Atlantic had pounded it to rubble, a place where luxurious yachts with brightly colored pennants had come bearing guests and finery.

To the credit of the National Park Service, Cumberland Island has finally been made a National Seashore and will be kept as a wilderness and a relic of old and happy times along the southern coast. Now, however, there are pressures for permanent access points from the mainland, so more tourists can enjoy it. So far these have been resisted, for the end result would be erosion, vandalism, and the inevitable litter of crowds who do not understand the real meaning of the island. Today they come by thousands, landing at temporary piers, and it saddens me to consider what the end of this lovely and mysterious place will be. I wonder what Sidney Lanier would think. He would mourn the change, and perhaps members of Congress and the National Park Service would be swayed by his testimony.

If it could be kept as it once was, Cumberland would be worth far more as a sanctuary of the spirit, and future generations would bless those who had the foresight to set it aside. Cumberland Island qualifies for an honored position in those places throughout the world which have come to mean something in the hearts of men. I have not been back since my first visit, and sometimes it is best never to go back but remember it as it was.

Mavericks

A maverick is one who does not fit into the commonplace as others do, nor fall into the expected mold: a stray animal that doesn't want to run with the herd. In this vein, I often think of Jack London and his stories of the gold rush of 1898 in Alaska. He not only climbed the terrible and killing trail over the White Pass but guided boats and rafts down the dangerous rapids of the Yukon River below Whitehorse, Alaska. He found no gold, but instead wrote the story *White Fang,* and many other books, later translated into foreign languages all over the world. A brawling two-fisted type, he welcomed any battle, be it a free-for-all or a solitary one. Once, in a bar on the San Francisco waterfront called the Barbary Coast, I enjoyed imagining he was still there.

As Robert Service, the bard of the Yukon, sang:

> There's a race of men that don't fit in,
> A race that can't stay still;

So they break the hearts of kith and kin,
    And they roam the world at will.
They range the field and they rove the flood,
    And they climb the mountain's crest;
Theirs is the curse of the gypsy blood,
    And they don't know how to rest. . . .

He's a rolling stone, and it's bred in the bone;
    He's a man who won't fit in.

There are gentle types of mavericks who scorn and avoid conflicts, such as John Burroughs. In his studio at Slabsides near the Hudson River, he wrote many beautiful books on birds, flowers—everything he saw. Generations of schoolchildren have made pilgrimages to his old home, walking down the paths and finding nests of warblers and thrushes as he did.

James Oliver Curwood, with his romantic stories of brave Canadian Mounted Police in their gaudy uniforms, intrigued me as a boy and shaped my own life of exploration and adventure in the Northwest Territories.

Bob Marshall, whom I knew well, climbed all the major peaks of the Adirondacks and extended his operations into the West and North far into Alaska, where he spent a year exploring and mapping the formidable Brooks Range. His book about that time of his life, *Arctic Village,* has affected the preservation of our last frontier, a battle raging at this moment. A trained forester with the Department of Agriculture, Bob made decisions that were respected. He was an indomitable man who loved to take hikes, some forty-five miles a day, both to demonstrate his hardiness and because he enjoyed them. I made several trips with him and know now that his early death at thirty-nine must have been due to overexertion.

Justice William O. Douglas of the United States Supreme Court was somewhat of a maverick. Not only was he a great justice, who might have been President of this country, but he fought for wilderness wherever it was threatened. I was with him along the Potomac east of Washington, D.C., and hiked one hundred and eighty miles from Cumberland, Maryland, down the canal route to its end, a well-publicized effort that resulted in the river being set aside as a National Historic Park. When I made a canoe trip with him in the Quetico-Superior country, he was offered the red carpet treatment by the U.S. Forest Service, which he refused, preferring to paddle nearly fifty miles to the landing at Winton, Minnesota, rather than take a pleasant motorboat ride.

Will Dilg, organizer of the Izaak Walton League of America, was another man in a class by himself. After helping to set aside the Upper Mississippi River Wild Life and Fish Refuge to save the smallmouth bass (which he called "the fightin'est fish that swims") he turned his attention to the Boundary Waters Canoe Area. In the early 1920's I guided his party, which included several photographers, writers like Don Hough of the *Saturday Evening Post,* Charley Heddon, a famous fisherman and tackle manufacturer, and others. I remember sitting around a campfire on Ottertrack Lake on the Canadian border when he said, "The Izaak Walton League will devote its energies to the preservation of the wilderness canoe country." This pledge was honored through all its subsequent battles, including the latest one, which resulted in the Boundary Waters being declared a Wilderness Area in an act signed by President Carter in 1978.

Will was a strange and uncompromising man, dictatorial and ruthless with those who opposed him. He was somewhat careless about details of management, but he accomplished a great deal and fostered a spirit that spurred the league to take on conservation projects all over the country.

What means most to me, however, is the inspiration from mavericks long dead and gone, like Zane Grey, who wrote of the deserts of the Southwest. I can smell the sage, see the colorful mountains of New Mexico and Arizona, live with the Navajos and the Hopis in their sacred canyons and at their waterholes.

Ernest Thompson Seton also knew the Southwest, but he was more at home in the far north of Canada. A great artist, he roamed everywhere, studying and sketching the animals of the forests and tundras. His work was accurate in intimate detail and no aspect of life was ever neglected. I have a complete collection of his beautiful books—*Wild Animals I Have Known* and others—and treasure them for their vast knowledge and artistry.

Another set of books I read as a young boy were the adventures of Joseph Alexander Altsheler. My imagination went rampant as I joined him in *The Riflemen of the Ohio* and *The Dark and Bloody Ground.* I remember ecstatic times curled up in a hidden corner, thrilled by the dangers of Indians, wild beasts, and renegades. Even today when I fly over Ohio, Indiana, and Kentucky, I do not see a checkerboard of farms, towns, and cities; the land is, in my imagination, as it used to be in all its virgin glory. Altsheler made me a maverick in heart and soul.

One of the really great mavericks was Henry David Thoreau, who influenced me strongly. I read his *Walden, or Life in the Woods,* and the essays of the Merrimack River and the Adirondacks, and took his life-style as my own. For years I carried one of his books with me wherever I went and can still quote from many of his classic essays on simplicity and living off the land; I treasure his words: "In wildness is the preservation of the world." As have many other people, I have adopted his philosophy and made it mine.

Like all mavericks, the men I have mentioned preferred to be different, to run their own lives as they saw them; not to live in quiet desperation, but, as Thoreau advised, to approach the end knowing they had lived wisely. They lived fearlessly to the end and left their mark upon the world. No crowds in the marketplaces of civilization for them; instead the quiet of the wilderness or of the mind. This is what they sought, each one shaped by his beliefs and the environment in which he lived.

Boulders

It was long ago, when making a glaciological survey with a noted geologist, Dr. Wallace Atwood, that I first became conscious of how great glaciers formed the land. From the air we saw how those enormous ice sheets had moved like giant rasps from the Northeast to the Southwest, changing the courses of rivers, gouging out the basins of lakes, scouring out rocky basins as though they were made of putty. I was impressed by his enthusiasm (he was then in his seventies) and the excitement he found in new specimens on the ground as well as in seeing the whole broad view of the cataclysms that had occurred long ago.

That is why the huge boulders, those scraping tools of the ice, have always interested me and inspired me with the story they told. In them is the history of mankind's struggle to survive the monumental ice sheets that once covered all the land. Man could do nothing to stem the flow of the ice, but when the warmth returned he followed along its lower edges as did all forms of life, with good hunting everywhere for mammoths, giant deer, and moose. The threatening presence of bears, wolves, and carrion hunters kept him alert to danger. Modern man has not forgotten these struggles, for imprinted on his subconscious mind is the picture of those violent days of the past.

On the shore of the lake where I have my cabin there are many boulders resting on smaller stones dropped onto the ledges of the ancient Precambrian base over which the glaciers rode. One of the boulders is near the cabin, and I marvel at the balance that has not been disturbed for over ten thousand years. These glacial boulders are called erratics, and I can see in my mind's eye the countless millions of them scattered all over the North, the legacy of the great cold that swept down time and again over a million years.

When I sit in my canoe before one of these boulders now, I envision ancient hunters, the thrill and excitement of the kills, women helping with preparation of the meat, the feasting and joy. I can see the fires roasting huge chunks of meat, hunters being given the choice parts, the liver and entrails, as is the custom among primitive peoples even today. Our roots go deep, very deep, and it takes only an expedition after game to bring them to consciousness.

Not long ago I watched a bear-hunting party in northern Wisconsin making elaborate preparations for their foray into the wilds. The men had driven into a small neighborhood garbage dump where black bears were accustomed to come for food. They had dogs with them and there was much drinking and boasting of the great hunts they had had together. After a period of waiting for the moon to come out, they turned the dogs loose and for a few hours escaped the humdrum of the lives they had left behind. This was distasteful to me, for

I do not approve of this kind of hunting, yet I understood and recognized their common bond with the hunters of the past.

After a while I heard a fusillade of rifle fire and knew the dogs had found a bear. Soon there was the sound of men and dogs approaching, dragging a bloody carcass over the snow, all with much shouting and laughter. One of them started the truck as the trophy was heaved in the back, followed by the pack of dogs. The men piled in with them and off they went into the night. I could hear the racket for a mile and then all was still as they roared into a bar to boast of their adventure.

Soon after this episode I flew over the area south of my home as far as Lake Superior and studied the terrain and the ancient paths of glacial rivers. I looked over old glacial ponds that once were full of meltwater, studied the encroaching ring of sphagnum and heather, the tamarack and black spruce moving out from the center as the surface covering grew dry enough to support them. And so it has been all over the North, the lakes gouged out by the ice, the boulders scattered everywhere—all souvenirs of the ice ages the world has known. All this the erratics brought to life, each reminding me, "Look well, modern man, look well and ponder, don't forget."

How does one accommodate modern existence with its luxuries and artificialities into the broad spectrum of a past when our ancestors fought for their lives against the inexorable flow of the ice, changing climates, and migrations? All one can say is that knowledge of the past makes the present richer and more meaningful. If wholeness and awareness are the true goals of existence, perhaps this is part of the truth we have been seeking.

A Time
of Dryness

The cycles of drought and abundant moisture can never be fully accounted for or explained, for they have to do with such things as sunspots and stratospheric aberrations. High global winds, carrying the pollution of our industrialized earth—carbon monoxide, nitrous oxides and monoxides, and other by-products—are also known to have an effect on the cycles. We speak glibly of the phenomena of the Van Allen Belt, the greenhouse effect, and the cooling of the earth's surface without understanding their significance.

No one really knows why the glaciers overrode much of the planet, leaving devastation in their wake over millions of years, and why there were interglacial periods when the ice retreated. Perhaps the vastness of the oceans with their tides and shifting currents caused the movement, releasing moisture to a lush and verdant world and then withholding it, spreading dryness over huge areas where once were the gardens of Eden. There are deserts on the march and millions have suffered starvation and death as the result of their inexorable advance. We read about this and ponder, but it is always so far away it seems unreal, something that could never happen to us.

However, when the drought came to our area we were appalled and old assurances crumbled in the face of reality. We became aware of the creeping signs with alarm, the river leading out of the bay below my cabin on Listening Point going dry from bank to bank and water lilies dying in the shallows, the feeding ground for ducks, blue herons, and muskrats. The sand beach near the sauna was many feet from the old shoreline, now a bed of black muck and debris.

It was on the highlands we first noticed what was really happening. The blueberries, caribou moss, and bearberry were shriveling; rock ferns, arbutus, clintonia, and goldthread flowers were turning brown; but it was the pines and spruces growing over the old Precambrian granite, schist, and greenstone that were really in trouble. For two years we watched them turn almost a rust color, first the tops, then lower down. If only the rains had come they might have survived, but the rains did not come.

The old trees stood bare and sere and we saw them die, a sad thing, for we had listened to the wind moaning through their high branches, the kinglets and nuthatches singing their songs there. Now all of this was gone; the only happy birds were the pileated woodpeckers, who swiftly discovered the harbored beetles and grubs in the dead trees. Each day we heard their loud wicker-wicker-wicker as they soared in to the harvest, then the rapid tattoo as they cut huge holes in their search for food.

At last the rains came in torrential blasts that threatened to wash the soil from the rocks. High winds followed and some of the trees were washed out and fell, and still it rained. After a time the parched soil and humus began to soak up the moisture and hold it. My little spring-fed well, which had been dry, soon filled to overflowing. The mosses, ferns, and flowers freshened, and seeds that had lain dormant sprang to life.

The frogs, even the big bullfrogs in the pool along the trail from the sauna to the cabin, came back, and I could hear their harumph-harumph echoing in the night. The lake filled swiftly, and soon the desiccated beach was back to normal and we could enjoy the clean white sand. A pair of ducks built a nest close to the cabin and another beyond the beach to the south.

We had waited long for this joyous time. Then came the snows and the land was covered with a heavy blanket of white, hiding the devastation of the drought years. In the spring it seemed as though nothing had happened; the mosses were just as lush and the berries grew fresh green stems.

However, there is an open space where the pines died, and we can see through where once there was a solid bank of green. Young trees are beginning to grow, but we shall never see them as they were.

Time had dealt harshly with Listening Point, but the land was still there and for a while it would not change; in the grand cycles of the seasons and the years to come no one would know what had happened. The dead pines would become part of the soil, adding their substance to it, sturdy trees would take their place with the flowers and birds, and all would be forgotten.

The Scourge

We first became aware of the infestation of forest tent caterpillars during the summer of 1978. We had already been through the time of dryness and thought our troubles had ended. The worms came in quietly without warning and we could see the aspen and even the birch were being eaten at the tops. We were reminded of the summer thirty years before when they were so thick the trains on the Canadian National Railway could not make the grade because the rails were so slippery with caterpillars, and in some areas cars skidded on the highways. I was at Grand Portage on Lake Superior that summer making a survey for the Department of the Interior, and the woods were almost impassable with webs hanging from the brush and trees.

Now the scourge was with us again. It reminded me of locust plagues in the Bible and how whole populations died of starvation as all their crops were eaten. The local inhabitants knew they had sinned and all this was punishment from a wrathful God. We have had similar plagues of grasshoppers in modern times with the same result, and we know of the spread and destruction by the chestnut blight in eastern forests and by the spruce budworm and Dutch elm disease everywhere.

I went out to Listening Point one day and the worms were crawling over the cabin, hanging festooned from the trees and on the sauna dock. They had stripped the trees and I wondered if the woods would survive a second defoliation.

I knew the scourge would be with us until the three-year cycle had finished its work and the worms had gone into a state of dormancy or decline due to their natural enemy, a large blackfly. I also knew they would return when the time was ripe and they had a chance to recoup their strength as a species. Fortunately there will be a period of respite before they come back, and like all other catastrophies they have their place in time. All we helpless humans can do is accept it.

The spruce budworm has killed uncountable numbers of trees in northern forests, and now their trunks are covered with moss, rotting and falling into the forest cover. The dead trees become a fire hazard and center of disease. Spraying has been tried and many thousands of dollars spent, but to no avail.

In the New England states we lost great stands of native chestnut. The trees would come back from seed or roots, grow to a certain size, then wither and die for no apparent reason. No forest research team has found an answer, and as a result the forest ecology has been changed for both flora and fauna.

The Dutch elm disease has destroyed beautiful colonnades of trees in many hundreds of cities and towns in the Midwest. Once a very popular tree in urban areas, the elm has gradually disappeared in spite of everything we have done to try to stop the ravages. The disease is so dangerous it is difficult to dispose of dead elms for fear of contamination elsewhere. I have seen cities stark and bare where, before the onslaught, those great

trees with their welcome shade and loveliness made approaches sheer delight. Only the unsightly stumps and ugliness remained. New species such as maple and oak have been planted, but it took centuries for the old elms to mature and none of us will live to see them grow again.

Another scourge was the white-pine blister rust, which caused the pines to lose their needles. Thirty years ago it was predicted there would not be a white pine left by the turn of the century, and again large sums were spent to combat the invasion and eliminate those trees disfigured by the blisters which formed in the bark. Gooseberry and currant bushes were intermediate hosts, and during the Civilian Conservation Corps days lines of workers instructed to kill all such shrubs were sent into stricken forests.

Much research was done in selecting seed from rust-free trees, then planting and grafting the young seedlings onto other young trees with established roots. The work is still being continued and may never end, but the white pine has not disappeared as a valuable forest resource and will possibly survive.

The red-pine terminal borer is also a devastating parasite. Although the situation has never been as desperate as the one concerning the white pine, it is significant because the white and red pine grow together and some experts wonder if there is any correlation between the two threats.

There are far lesser evils which attack man and make life in the North rather unbearable during certain months of the year. Blackflies are the worst, for they draw blood with every bite, and infections from them have actually driven men wild. They hover over shorelines and along rivers, a hazard to canoeists. No-see-ums, or biting midges, insects about as big as a pencil point, make one suffer with their bite and itch and,

unlike mosquitoes, attack silently. Mosquitoes can be controlled with mosquito-proof tents and bug spray. At dusk and
on wet or cloudy days they are most ferocious, and woe to
the man who lets one into his tent—he will be serenaded most
of the night.

These are minor scourges when compared to the big ones,
but, as someone said, they must have a purpose, for they are
God's creatures as much as we. I wondered about this until a
friend of mine, Bob Drexler, who was doing his doctorate
thesis on mosses and lichens, discovered that mosquitoes polli-
nate mosses. Who knows, perhaps someone will find that God
has a plan for blackflies, no-see-ums, horseflies, and deerflies.

The day before going out to Listening Point we had driven
down the North Shore route to Lake Superior, and noticed the
trees on either side of the highway completely defoliated, as
bare as though it were winter. We were heartsick, for we had
been in Wisconsin, which was still untouched. All this had
happened in the two weeks we were away. We turned north
from the town of Two Harbors near the big lake, and for ten
or fifteen miles it was the same; then the infestation began to
taper off until it looked as though the defoliation had stopped.
Encouraged by this, we looked forward to going to the Point
on our return.

As we drove up the road to Listening Point in early July
we could see our optimism had been misplaced, for even the
black ash in the swamps were stripped. We looked at it all with
dismay, but there was one good thing to consider—the worms
would not last more than another two weeks.

All catastrophies disappear and are forgotten over the
years, for that is the way of life. We remember what they were
like and smile ruefully at what they did to us. As I have said,
the land is still there and, taken in perspective, it is not so

bad. As with expeditions into the wilds when we have endured storms and rapids, cold and sleet, and sometimes lack of food, it is ultimately the good things we remember, not the bad. With that conclusion we should be able to face any future catastrophe.

Tornado

Tornadoes are frightening, and news that one is on its way strikes fear into the hearts of anyone in its path, as those know who live in the tornado belt and have seen what they can do to towns, cities, farms, and forests. Such awe-inspiring disasters can be matched only by the flooding of major rivers' lowlands, by earthquakes, or by the devastation of war.

All this was in my thoughts as I traveled the tornado belt of western Minnesota. Walking across the prairie one hot summer afternoon when the heat waves shimmered on the horizon, I thought of the farmers who had dug cyclone cellars under their homes for a safe retreat should the warnings come. If far from home they sought shelter in ditches or arroyos, creek banks, or any place they could find away from the powerful winds, often a hundred miles an hour. In a sense it was like going into a bomb shelter during the war when the sirens started screaming. This was a matter of survival; they were familiar with the warnings.

Suddenly I was aware of a deathly calm and growing darkness and I knew instinctively what was going to happen. Then I saw it half a mile away, the black swirling cone of a real twister; the top was brown and mushroom shaped with a long dark tail reaching to the ground. I watched as the tip of the funnel drew up debris wherever it touched. I looked around for a place to hide but there was nothing, only flat prairie. I chose a spot and began to dig deep enough with my hands so my body would be level with the ground. To my relief it veered and headed off into the distance to dissipate its wrath.

After that experience I went back to my own country, which was usually out of the tornado belt. One evening in September, after the summer of the drought, the sky grew dark quickly, with the same ominous calm I remembered from the cyclone in the West. This time the winds were followed by slashing rain; I imagined the lake by my cabin was in violent turmoil. I had no thought of what was really going on, for we happened to be on a different part of the lake, just north of the cabin, but I should have read the signs. Because it was late and stormy we decided not to stay overnight and went back to town instead.

That night over the radio we learned many areas had been struck by a tornado. Islands had been denuded of trees and houses destroyed, some deaths had resulted from falling trees on Basswood Lake, and an airplane had overturned on White Iron Lake near Ely. All this made us wonder what had happened at Listening Point and we drove out early the next morning.

As we approached the Point we could see the damage, trees down and twisted, blocking the road to the cabin. We chopped and hacked our way through to the turnaround and found the

trail to the cabin was a crisscross of broken treetops, a jackstraw
puzzle of tangled debris. It was unbelievable; I looked at the
trees, remembering how over the years we had treasured each
one of them. We cut our way in with axes and saws and when
we finally reached the cabin, we were greatly relieved to see
it had not been touched, though all around was chaos. When
friends came we all worked unceasingly until the paths were
clear. We learned our closest neighbors had spent the night in
their cabin in the very midst of crashing trees, not knowing
if one would crush their little house. We would have experienced the same thing had we not gone to our home in
town.

Our son Robert and his wife, Yvonne, called the next day,
having heard the news, and when we told them of our plight
they came from Wisconsin and spent several days continuing
what we had begun. A huge Norway pine had fallen just north
of the cabin, upturning a black mass of roots and precious
topsoil, stripping from the smooth surface of the bedrocks all
the mosses and lichens, blueberry plants, linnaea, bearberry,
and dwarf dogwood. I looked at this with sadness, for these
were special friends. Robert had an inspiration: why not cut
the base of the log as close to the stump as possible? Noting
that if cut at a certain angle the fallen trunk might spring back
into place, he proceeded with the cut, watching carefully as
it opened just as he had hoped. Then like a miracle, as he threw
himself aside to keep from being struck by the root mass, it
dropped neatly into the exact spot from which it had been
torn. We were astounded, for the mosses and flowers were just
as they were before. We hurried to the lake and carried many
buckets of water to soak down the soil that had so rudely been
torn away.

Then came the slow process of repairing other damage. We

were thankful the cabin, woodpile and woodshed, sauna and dock were all right, so we tackled the work of salvaging the wood we could, rolling the biggest logs into the brush where they would rot and go back to the soil. I sometimes wonder about the meaning of such things as this tornado—why it happened, why it leapfrogged over some areas and hit others. We paddled to the islands beyond Listening Point and saw where many trees had been blown over, all old landmarks along the shore. They would lie there for many years until they, too, would sink into the soil and disappear.

Little Rivers

Little rivers, beautiful, wild, and clear, meander through my dreams. They have no waterfalls so their generation of power is not worth selling. Only flowers are along their banks, and in boggy places are soft depths of sphagnum mosses, yellow cowslips, and blue-flags erect and gay. There is the rich pungence of cedar and damp earth. In the mornings one can hear the long thrilling call of white-throated sparrows, and at dusk the nighthawks zoom overhead.

A marvelous quality of little rivers is the native brook trout living in them—*Salvelinus fontinalus,* the most beautiful fish in the world, at least to me. I have always thought that brookies, with their brilliantly mottled sides and red spots aflame along their bellies, were far too lovely to eat, but to my grandmother, who understood how I felt about trout fishing, it was entirely different. She helped me get ready for my first fishing trip, gave me some of her strongest thread for fishline, and went into a nearby tamarack swamp to help

Little Rivers

me select a springy specimen for a pole. She watched as I peeled off the bark, still full of sap, and polished it a golden brown.

After the day's fishing on Dead Man's Creek it was getting dark. She and I washed my fish under the pump outside the kitchen door, dried them with a clean towel, and sprinkled them with flour and salt. She knew exactly what to do. Grandmother laid them side by side in the frying pan in golden, sizzling butter, and we watched those brookies change from crimson-dotted green to something that delighted my boyish eyes. I have told the story before of how we sat down under the light of the kitchen lamp, at a table spread with a red-and-black checkered cloth, to a feast of trout and milk, with freshly baked bread, an eighty-year-old lady and a boy of twelve, to talk of robins and spring, and the eternal joy of fishing.

Even today those memories are precious to me, for this was one of the first little rivers I knew where I lived in Wisconsin. They were all very small and shallow; most were narrow enough to jump across, but there were always logs piled helter-skelter from the logging days, black rotting logs covered with moss. Those miniature dams had dark mysterious recesses underneath them where brook trout lurked and waited for me.

Mosquito Brook was somewhat similar to Dead Man's Creek, but with a significant difference as the name implies. In a swampy lowland or on dank and muggy days, the mosquitoes, sandflies, and no-see-ums all but ate you alive. The few fish I took there, however, were large and worth all the suffering I endured.

Bruns Willow was the creek of the golden sands, where it seemed as though trout stole some of the color from the sand itself. I can still see that golden bottom shining in the sunshine and used to feel just being there was the most wonderful thing in the world.

The Totogatik was an exciting stream much larger than the others with more variety and challenge. There was a meadow where grasses grew tall, almost hiding the river from view as it wound through its devious channel. Under such conditions one must approach warily and with finesse, drop the bait to the unseen surface. One never had long to wait, for almost instantly and without warning would come a violent slap as a monster took the lure, usually a freshly caught grasshopper or an angleworm dug out of the bank. Then a sharp jerk on the line and a beauty would lie among the tussocks thrashing around as it tried desperately to return to the haven from which it came.

Once I found a tributary of the Totogatik, a tiny creek with a big pool I knew must be full of trout. A shelf of rock overlooked the pond and from it I could look down into crystal-clear water. At the far end was a bit of sand where the creek flowed in, and around were enormous trees, yellow birch, hemlock, and pine. Here in such solitude and beauty I sensed there was a corner of primitive America unseen and untouched except by me.

The Nemakagon was a famous stream and because I lived nearby, I knew it well. Its waters were deep and cold and I fished pools where at dusk big trout were rising everywhere. On this river, I was taught to use a fly rod by an old-timer who scorned the use of any kind of bait. A dry fly with a tapered leader, he told me, was the mark of a man. I'll never forget the day I learned to skitter a fly across a riffle, making the lure look exactly like an escaping insect, and, what is more important, caught a nice one. The old-timer would have laughed if he had watched me.

My later years in Minnesota were entirely different from the early ones in Wisconsin, but my love of trout fishing remained unchanged; I found the sport more exciting than ever. Longstaff Creek, tumbling down from a rocky, pine-grown canyon, was one that rated high in my affections. I used to hike along an old trail on dewy mornings to reach the highlands from which it sprang. How that creek flashed in the sunshine as it dashed over the rocks and pebbles on its way to the valley! It held no big ones, but it gave me a special joy to be there.

The Baptism River had a series of big pools one after the other connected by short sparkling rapids that in themselves were a challenge with a fly rod. As I worked my way down this complex of water I was sure to take my limit of good-sized and well-colored trout. The river's name intrigued me. Why was it called the Baptism? Was it part of the legend of early missionaries to the Indians? I decided perhaps a baptism had taken place at the river during the days of exploration. I never knew for sure, but the thought made my trips there more interesting.

The Manitou was a quiet winding stream reached after several miles of scrambling through brush and over windfalls in rough and boulder-strewn land. Once I filled my creel without moving downstream as I usually did. It was always worthwhile making the trip, for the trout were large and fought more tenaciously than anywhere else.

There is a little campsite on the Isabella River, a stream I knew better, perhaps, than any of the others. My old fishing pals Glenn and Dean, who went there with me, are long gone, but I like going back there to visit with them, for their spirits are with me. From the old overgrown campsite in a scrubby stand of jackpine and spruce, the whitethroats call as they used to. The tree is still there where we hung our rods, and I hear the happy banter of long ago.

These are a few of the little rivers I have known, all different but never changing. Those lovely trout flash through my memories as vividly today as when I caught my first.

Trees
of the Forest

Trees of the forest have many strange associations. Cedars and birches grow together, and seem to have an affinity for each other with the same ecological requirements; no doubt born through the alchemy of fires which swept through the country during seasons of drought, their partnership is a unique one.

Another peculiarity is that cedars usually grow in swampy areas but are also found on rocky cliffs far from the water they prefer, and grow everywhere as birches do along the borders of beaver flowages and along the crests of ridges. A symbiotic pair, they carry great cultural significance for the Indian tribes of the continent.

Beneath the white-barked trees blueberries and other fruits grow, and in bogs they border are golden stands of wild rice. Mahnomen, the name the Indians gave this delicacy, brings back a vision of birches standing tall and straight around the harvest fields. As the Indians push their way in birchbark canoes through the ripened rice, flocks of ducks hover over them, fat and slow after gorging themselves and easy to kill with sticks or paddles. They will go into the pots with the rice cooking over many little fires.

Where does cedar come into the scene? Without it there would have been no canoe, the greatest primitive invention for travel the northland has ever known. Thin, carefully split lengths of cedar were used to line the fragile birch bark on the inside, giving canoes lightness enough to portage. It was the birchbark canoe that opened up the vast network of the waterways. Indians built small canoes for hunting, twelve to fourteen feet in length, North canoes of twenty-five feet for the interior lakes, and the huge Montreals up to thirty-five feet for the storms on the Great Lakes, where winds and waves could tear a canoe apart.

Manned by twelve to fourteen men, these enormous crafts carried loads of many tons, bales of fur, trade goods, food, and supplies, until at times the gunwales were only a few inches above the water. They were the basis of the fur trade, the Indians and voyageurs the power that moved them on their way.

Cedar is of great significance in foreign lands as well, and we must not forget the cedars of Lebanon, where now only a small grove remains of the vast forests of the past. King Solomon built his temple to Jehovah, God of the Hebrews, with those cedars, inlaying the wood with gold and precious stones. Thus began the denuding of the mountainsides where these magnificent trees had flourished for many centuries.

Following King Solomon's example, in moved the merchants, or loggers as we would call them, and the redolent cedars became an important article of commerce throughout the entire Mediterranean region. What the logging began, goats and sheep finished by eating the shrubs and grasses right down to the ground. With absolutely no cover, erosion set in and millions of square miles of once verdant country became barren and unproductive.

I think of our own huge stands of cedar on the West Coast, extending from California to British Columbia and along the scenic inside passage sweeping into the Yukon and Alaska. Today these groves supply lumber for housing and other products, not only in the United States and Canada, but other nations. In the Quetico-Superior country cedars have reached the age of seven hundred and fifty years and in the Far West, several thousand years, some dating back to before the birth of Christ.

Big maples provided sugar in the spring, with whole families departing for the sugar bush when the golden sap was running. There was snow on the ground and the earth was coming alive. Children were always there during the sugaring to pick up frozen droplets when buckets spilled. Geese were on the move and it was a joyous time. Maple sugar was used with wild rice and sometimes with pemmican, a mixture of fat and pounded meat. Stored in waterproof bags, maple sugar was an essential item to fur traders in the northwestern prairies of Canada.

The spruce tree provided long tough fibers in its roots which were used in canoe making in the spring. With them Indian women sewed strips of pliable birch bark together and sealed them with resin from balsam, spruce, or pine to make the canoe waterproof. When the men were gone on hunting expeditions or at war, they carried a pitch pot and if there was a leak, inevitable in rough country, they could boil the contents and smear it over a tear. This was a nightly ritual of the voyageurs, who took care of a canoe by the light of a campfire.

The forests provided many kinds of food, especially nuts.

When the leaves were in full color and the forest floor rustling with them, the scene was set for the harvest. There were hazelnuts growing on low bushes and easy to reach; walnuts, butternuts, hickory nuts, or acorns from the oaks, which meant a different kind of gathering. Young men climbed the tall trees, shaking the laden branches to bring the fruits to earth, but it was usually a matter of waiting until they fell to the ground. Then it was a race to see who got them first, the squirrels, raccoons, bears, or wild turkeys.

If the nuts were not ripe they would be placed on mats in the sun or, if the weather was rainy and foul, beside open fires to ready them for the cracking and the important task of picking out the meat. This valuable food, rich in oil and protein, was stored in birchbark containers and treasured against the long barren winters when people needed something extra to supplement a diet of venison, moose, or fish.

When I think of the beauty of the forest as the Indians knew it, I come to share their belief that its trees grew there through the generosity of the Great Spirit. Being of the Great Spirit the trees were accepted as His gifts with humbleness and gratitude. Thus we must guard, protect, and cherish them as the Indians did, so our children may have them forever.

The Hemlocks

Hemlocks have always held a special place in my affections, which may have stemmed from my early boyhood in Wisconsin. I had caught and tamed a pair of squirrels and, knowing they liked hemlock buds, kept a supply of fresh branches for them to enjoy. Now whenever I see a hemlock, those old memories spring forth.

The eastern hemlocks belong to Wisconsin, or so it seemed to me then. I recall during the first logging days that one of the big companies offered a thousand-dollar reward to anyone finding a hemlock in Minnesota. As far as I know the prize was never awarded.

When Elizabeth and I spent two months last winter at her old farm home in northern Wisconsin, I made the acquaintance of as many of those trees as I could find on the timbered reaches of the farm along the Namekagon River. All hemlocks thrive in places of rather poor drainage close to the water and the big cedars, but sometimes they grow on the highlands, great stands of them. One can never be sure. Years ago, one had grown along the river trail, but it had died. I found another a short distance away, a rather large one that had become a landmark for any further research.

I leaned against the one I had found and gazed at the long slender branches against the light, the graceful waving fronds, the seedpods at their ends, and the cracked grayish-brown trunk. North of the farm was once a large growth of old primeval hemlocks. I used to walk through it, repeating Longfellow's "Evangeline":

This is the forest primeval. The murmuring pines and the
    hemlocks . . .
Stand like druids of eld.

Now I decided to really begin a search, for surely there was more than one hemlock. I followed the river trail up into an opening where the snow was deep and looked out over the terrain. Hemlock number one was down in a valley, its roots deep in the moisture of a little creek with huge cedars and spruces all around.

Beyond the opening loomed a forest of pine. I snowshoed through an unbroken depth of white, zigzagging back and forth, searching for the elusive goal of another hemlock. About two hundred yards away my grandson Derek, who was with me, called excitedly, "One down here." I worked my way along his trail, and below the shelf we had been following in a little canyon, he proudly pointed to his find, another beautiful hemlock, the branches laden with snow. He broke off a branch tip and tossed it to me—the same kind of tips I used to put into my squirrel cage.

"Congratulations," I said, "this one's yours, hemlock number two."

Because it was getting late we hurried back along the path to the house nearly a mile away, but resolved to come back some day when the sun was shining. Elizabeth greeted us. "What luck?" she asked. I handed her the branch tip Derek had given me and she placed it in a little vase on the supper table.

A few days later we retraced our steps to the second hemlock and then worked our way closer to the Namekagon River, combing the area for the slightest hint of a sign. Now we were on familiar ground; where there was one there must be more. Circling and circling, we took separate routes, examining every tree that had the least resemblance to a hemlock, the trunk grayish brown, the slender drooping branches, and this time luck was with me. In a dense tangle of alder and spruce, hazel brush and windfalls, I spotted my prize, that unmistakable silhouette! Hemlock number three. We felt rather smug at our success and were determined to add as many more as we could.

Another day we searched tirelessly but found nothing so we edged our way to the east. We were happy to find hemlock number four, not as large as the first three, growing almost between the roots of a pine. Derek went ahead about two hundred yards and called that he had found number five, a small stunted hemlock under the gloom of tall white pines and Norways.

We searched many times after that but were never successful. Evidently we had found them all, but we continued to look and dream. I never drive down a road in the hemlock country without watching and hoping, and maybe praying just a little, even though most of those roads have not borne hemlocks for a long time. We had found our five on the farm, and in the process the trees had taken on more meaning.

Lutra canadensis

Lutra canadensis, the otter, is a beautiful creature, lithe of body
with a long tapering tail. It has five toes, and webbed forefeet,
for it is a water animal and swims like the fish on which it
preys. Its legs are short, the underside of the feet hairy, to more
easily grasp slippery stones during the summer and ice in the
winter.

The pelage is glossy brown, dark and rich in tone, slightly
grayish on legs and cheeks, with the underside somewhat
lighter in color. Much prized over many centuries, the soft
underfur gives it warmth, the outer coat brilliance and glow.
Wars have been fought for it, natives subjugated and enslaved,
especially by the Russians of Alaska and along the British
Columbia coast and elsewhere. Natives were always urged to
bring in the precious pelts.

The otter is a large mammal, forty to forty-five inches in
length, weighing from eighteen to twenty-five pounds. Various other species, such as the sea otter of the Pacific Coast,

are larger and heavier. Wherever it is found, its appeal is supreme and is matched only by the sable. All the various breeds are important and the great fur companies vied with each other to bring in as many as possible. Though during the fur trade era on this continent the beaver for a time was paramount, for sheer beauty there was no pelt to compare with the otter's.

The otter ranges through most of North America and Siberia, feeding on fish and crayfish, and sometimes birds and small mammals such as ducks and muskrats. Its three or four young are born in April in a den in a dirt bank with an underwater entrance like the beaver's. Never far distant from lakes and streams, it will travel considerable distances to find open water, especially in the winter.

This animal has survived the forays of many different predators. A courageous fighter, it can crush a dog's leg or that of other enemies such as a wolf or even a wolverine. It uses subterfuge and cleverness in its constant search for food. I have seen an otter swim out to a mother duck with a flock of ducklings around her, swimming all the way under water, and snatch a member of the unsuspecting family, before swimming back to shore. The maneuver was repeated until the hunter had enough for its own young.

Two of the most appealing characteristics of *Lutra canadensis* are its playfulness and the fact it is easily tamed and shows no great fear of humans. During the winter otters often come up quite near to us to feed and play and I have seen them cavorting alone or with their families. Their legs tucked safely at their sides, they take turns sliding down a slope leaving a long shallow groove in the snow. In the summer they slip down smooth clay banks well lubricated by the water, playing like children.

They often make a sniffing or hissing sound as they tread water, and I am sure if there are young around this is a warning signal. I recall a trip into the Quetico with a friend, Bob Cooney, who wanted more than anything to photograph wild otters. We were camped on Robinson Lake quite near a sand beach where I had seen them on several occasions.

We paddled over and approached the shore cautiously but there was no otter in sight. A big flat rock lay to one side of us and we stopped to rest, the canoe nestled against the boulder. Suddenly we heard a scratching sound on the flat surface of the rock and saw three young ones disporting themselves; they were scratching their hides, rolling over, playing like little scalawags, having the time of their lives. My partner turned in horror and realized he had forgotten his camera in the hurry of getting away from camp. He gave me a desperate and woebegone look, watching the otters in dismay. To make it even more of a tragedy, the mother otter came up right behind the canoe and whistled to her babies. One by one they dove into the water, swimming under and around us, showing no fear whatsoever. Then they swam back to the beach and the party was over.

Bob turned to me with the most frustrated look I have ever seen on a man's face.

"Well," I said, "at least you saw them. It may never happen again, but you've had an experience few woodsmen ever know. What's a picture? You have a memory and that's far more important."

Once on the Kawishiwi River, which is just east of my home, while we stopped for lunch, a full-grown otter appeared treading water about ten feet from us, making its usual alert, hissing noises and coming close enough so we could see its white whiskers and eyes. It cavorted around,

curious, and then dove, and we caught one glimpse of the dark glossy body.

The otter is the playboy of the North. We shall always look forward to its visits and the joy it brings to us and to wilderness travelers.

Campsites

Campsites are punctuation marks for a voyageur, signifying the end of the day. I may forget portages, rapids, and lakes, which merge into a nebulous montage of country traveled over, but there are some campsites that stand out vividly in my mind as special places remembered.

There are two sites near my home that have unusual significance. I used both in the autumn when leaves were ablaze. I recall a morning at Low Lake when it was calm and the color lay like a benediction over the land, a breathless scene when sounds seemed magnified and the silence overwhelming. I watched a trapper working on his woodpile and could hear the chuck-chuck of his ax as he split and piled the wood. The whole scene was cast in a shimmering glow. The other place was at the far east end of Garden Lake from which I could see wild rice standing golden and sere in the afternoon sun. Long after harvesting, those fields were still attracting ducks to feed on the kernels on the muddy bottom. The joy of watching them was compensation enough for the long trip in.

A campsite on the Isabella River was one I knew well, and close to one of the finest brook-trout streams of the area. The site was in a growth of jackpine and balsam; a rather grubby spot, but the ground was level and from a tent strung between two trees and facing the river's edge you could hear the chuckle of the water and, at dusk, the long lonesome call of a white-throated sparrow or a nighthawk.

McIntyre Lake in the Quetico-Superior has a wonderful campsite at the narrows on a smooth bare rock, with lake trout and walleye pike lying off the reefs in midsummer. Looking north and west you can see the sunsets and the moonrises south over the ridge toward Sarah Lake.

Joyce Lake to the east has an unusual quality. For some strange reason it appears to be overfull, higher in the center than at the shores. You get the feeling the lake is like a cup overflowing its rim. There are no sunrises or moonrises, for the body of water is hemmed by high ridges, but somehow no other spot in the world has this particular appeal.

Kashapiwigamack, a knifelike gash of a lake, has a campsite on its west shore. On a high cliff with several flat areas, one above the other, the campsite, wherever you pitch your tent, affords a north view of Cairn Lake. It is hard not to sense that in this place of mood and legendry is the spirit land of the Chippewas.

Southwest of Joyce is Robinson Lake, with a delightful campsite, a lovely strip of white sand to the north and a vista of a high cliff to the east. There is nothing to see here—no sunrises, as you are buried by the ridge—but fishing is excellent off a reef just beyond. The sun beats into this haven only at high noon and it is always immaculately clean (or was in the old days), and anyone there was careful to leave it that way. I recall a message left near the fireplace on a strip of birch bark which read, "Leave some kindling and wood here, and above all keep this beautiful place clean."

The Agnes Lake site at the south end has a magnificent view reaching many miles. The beginning of a vast complex of waterways branching off in all directions, it is a jumping-off place for adventure. What I remember best is the sun sparkling on the whitecaps.

On Bart Lake an island campsite is nestled against a stand of tall white pines with a fireplace at the water's edge where I used to build a live-box because the bass there were so plentiful. Sometimes they would jump over the rock enclosure, but they were easily replaced. Fly fishing was all we ever did there, and we often had two or three on at the same time and had to cut lines to untangle rods.

Lost Loon Lake is reached by a long rugged portage from Bart. Very few ever go there, for the brush is not cut and the windfalls are many. We like it that way because no one coming in would guess what lay to the north. The lake is not more than a quarter of a mile in length, but such bass fishing I have never seen. There were actually schools of large ones swimming beneath the canoes in the clear water. We named it Lost Loon Lake because a loon greeted us each time we went. Proof that no other fishermen knew our secret was confirmed years later when I returned and found the rocks of the old fireplace covered with lichen, the tent poles rotted, with no signs of intrusion.

Skull and Cross Bones Camp at the portage into Bart was given this frightening name because someone had tied the whitened skull of a moose and a couple of leg bones to a tree. It was not an attractive camp, an uneven place for a tent and fire, but we put up with it, for just fifty feet in front was a reef that produced walleyes and in the swampy bay with weeds and rushes lay enormous northern pike, often twenty to thirty pounds. It was a goal for all guides in those early days; some would stay there a week or more.

The campsite where the Darkey River runs to the north has a special mood appeal. It, too, is one of the spirit lakes of the Chippewa, where no one speaks when crossing. The Indians felt it was sacred, as they did Kashapiwigamack and the Kawishiwi. As proof of their belief they left some of the Quetico's finest pictographs there. The feeling of mystery pervades in the symbolism of their art.

Ottertrack Lake means much to me, for I camped there in the narrows on the first canoe trip I made into the Quetico. I was told by an Indian that if one studied the vertical rock on the north side, he could see otter tracks high up on the surface, but it was difficult to make out the prints unless the light was exactly right, and even then I was not sure. Nearby a cascading waterfall raced to the lake, and a short distance away was the gateway to Saganaga, which had great significance for me because few canoe men traveled that far from home. As a young guide it usually took me a week to get there and a week to return. We called it the great circle route. The campsite at the west end had just a hint of the broad sweep of Sag's waters, with its hundreds of islands stretching toward Cache Bay and Northern Light Lake, truly the gateway to the wilderness.

There are campsites in the Far North such as the Churchill just above Drum Rapids, where you listen to the beat of the drums, wondering what it will mean in the morning when the rapids must be faced with canoes and packs and whether we will measure up to its challenge.

I think of the Maligne River in Manitoba, of the drenching rains and torrential downpours with winds of hurricane force. We went into the willows for shelter and, sitting under ponchos, cowered like drowning rats. All this from a miserable campsite in a soggy muskeg with thunder and lightning to accentuate our plight.

These are some of the campsites I've known and loved. Scattered over North America they epitomize the joys and near disasters of the many trails I have followed in all seasons. These memories will forever make me grateful for the days when I roamed the bush like the coureur de bois I liked to imagine I was.

Friends
of the Trail

There are many friends of the trail I have met over the years, packing canoes over the portages, running the rapids, and camping with them all over the North. The memories I have of them are a comfort now that many have taken the trail over the last great divide. I should like to tell you about a few, and perhaps it will evoke memories of your own. My friends are from the border country; yours I can only guess at, but I am sure that, in whatever part of the world, they will be as cherished as mine.

Those who were with me on the little lakes south of Knife Lake on the border have a special place in my thoughts. One spring after a long, rough portage right after the ice went out, when the red-winged blackbirds were warbling in the swamps, what a joy it was when we finally arrived at the little lake where we had chosen to stop. Canoe men who travel only the regular routes have no idea what they are missing on the small lakes. Glen Lerch, Bill Croze, and I often camped on ledges, sometimes no more than a few hundred feet from the reefs where fish spawned. One day there was a blinding snowstorm so we built a big fire out of driftwood, cooked our meal, and enjoyed the whiteness around us. The trout were small, not more than two or three pounds, but fried to a golden brown over an open fire, they were something exceptional. That was a long time ago and I haven't been there since, but I know those little lakes are still full of trout and in the spring the blackbirds sing.

Wilson Carlson was a close friend and native of Ely. His shack in Hoist Bay on Basswood Lake was the base for many exciting activities. There was something unique about the shack, a certain atmosphere no other camp had. The bunks were filled with golden marsh grass cut in a swale nearby, and when you opened the door you inhaled the sweet smell of it. The huge oversized barrel stove salvaged from an abandoned logging camp almost filled the end of the cabin, but it took three-foot chunks of birch and aspen, which was a very important feature. When we returned from a cold and snowy day of hunting in the hills or in the blinds of Hoist Bay, there were always glowing coals that kept the shack warm while we were gone and could be fanned to life in a moment with a handful of dry birch bark or kindling.

Wilson was a happy and exuberant companion and did everything with gusto. During the hunting season he always got us up with the cry "Rise and shine!" Though it was four o'clock in the morning, we all knew he had been up an hour before that, mixing the batter for pancakes, frying thick slices of bacon, and brewing a pot of strong, black coffee, which stood simmering on top of the barrel stove. To him this was a joy, and those who were with him there over the years cherished the refuge he created from the world outside.

Wilson used to hang the deer on a long pole hung between two birches on one side of the trail leading up from the lake. He always hung them according to size; the ducks at either end got the same treatment, greenhead mallards first with their gorgeous plumage and then, toward the end of the season, the black and white bluebills. None of us will ever forget Wilson yelling out of the doorway into the dark, where we were getting our outfits together, "Come and get it before I throw it away!" These are only a few memories of all he did to make us happy there in the old shack, and now that he is gone, those of us who remain often think of him and all the fun we had.

During the early days of the Superior National Forest, I knew the rangers Tom Denley, Frank Carney, and Bill Barker. Wilson knew them too; they were the men who helped him get the discarded big stove for the shack. As a young naive guide I used to go down to the old Forest Service warehouse to watch them get ready for the summer's work. We talked about trails, portages, and fighting fires, which in those days broke out every year in the slashings during the dry periods. I worked with Tom Denley's crew north of Low Lake, and a tough fire boss he was. I helped patch the heavy, green canvas canoes, and on each side of the bow it was my job to paint the all-important letters U.S.F.S. We sharpened axes, fire-fighting tools such as mattocks and shovels, and other gear, anything that might be used in the months ahead.

As soon as the lakes were clear of ice, the rangers would start their travel and be gone most of the summer and into the fall. Sometimes they didn't get in until the lakes began to freeze, paddling in the teeth of the wind, driving sleet, and snow. Usually they came in once or twice to replenish food and other supplies or replace damaged equipment. Most of the time, however, they were on the lakes, clearing portages or looking for outlaws who might be stealing government timber or bringing in beaver hides out of season. After they finally returned it meant putting on snowshoes, setting up tents, and cruising timber during the bitter months of December through March, work they enjoyed in spite of the hardships.

Bill Trygg and his wife, Margaret, were also good friends, and he and I made many trips together in a canoe. What I remember most was Christmastime in their home overlooking a broad valley. At night we could see the lights of an iron ore mine fifteen miles away. During the holidays Bill was happiest, a perfect host to his many friends. No detail was ever forgotten in the Christmas preparations; there was even a swatch of fragrant balsam bough as a doormat for stomping off the snow. Bill's father, nearly ninety, was always there and what a treat to see him make potato, pork, and blood sausages and head-cheese the old-fashioned way for the feast days ahead. Of course no celebration was complete without the traditional mead of the Vikings.

Bill and Margaret are both gone now, but we shall never forget the glowing warmth of their holiday parties. Nor will we forget the lakes off of Knife, Wilson's shack, Pine Island, the men of the U.S. Forest Service, and many others, for memories of dear friends never die.

Those precious memories of our adventures will endure forever.

Predators

It was a wonderful sight to see the snowy owl, arrived from the barren lands several thousand miles away, sitting on a fence post perfectly satisfied with its perch. It had been driven south by the terrible storms of winter and the scarcity of food; its prey, lemmings and mice, were covered by a deep blanket of snow, and even ptarmigan, voles, and snowshoe hares were seldom seen. Instinctively the owl had taken off toward a land it knew was one of plenty. A long time ago I wrote a story about the snowy owl, and I can still see the beautiful creature, with its wingspread covering a double page, drawn by the great artist Charles Livingston Bull.

The other day on the trail to the cabin I found the remains of a partridge. The tail feathers were brown and black and I stuck one into my cap. This was the work of the great horned owl, another old friend. How many times I have listened to its who-who-who-hooooooooo at dusk and watched its deadly flight through the big pines. At roosting places I often pick up the pellets which tell the story of what it feeds on, along with bits of fur and fragments of bone and feathers.

The great horned owl chooses a hunting area where favorite game is close at hand. Its young are born in February, an impossible time of bitter cold here in the North, in nests built in a crotch or a hollow tree, and one wonders how the eggs hatch and how they survive. Its range is spread over most of the American continent, and when it soars through the moonlit woods and gives its dreaded call, all creatures freeze, waiting in terror until the marauder of the night has passed.

I recently saw a broad-winged hawk that lives near the beach below the cabin. I knew its young were there and unable to fly by the scream it emitted. The call was strange but unmistakable—like a peewee, but with more of a lisp perhaps: tsve-whee-eee, tsve-whee-weeeee. I looked up in the trees but could not see it again, and then I knew ventriloquism was the answer to the puzzle; the hawk would stay hidden until I left.

The broad-wing is a small hawk about the size of a crow, with none of the distinctive markings of some of the larger and gaudier hawks. It spends its life in the pines and thickets feeding on insects, small mammals, and birds, often sitting on the ground waiting for something to appear. Though rarely spectacular in its movements, during and after the breeding season it throws caution to the wind and joins others in large flocks soaring high above the terrain in a swooping pattern of diving flights like jet fighters zooming in for the kill. Up there in the bright blue sky the hawks seem to forget they are birds of glades and creeks. Down they come, free as the wind, swirling and turning in the brisk autumn breeze, then up once more and down again, playing a game only the broad-wings know.

All hawks are beautifully colored birds, whose flight swing-

ing low over a meadow is a sight to behold. Pirates of the breed, swift and maneuverable, they can drop in an instant to secure their prey. With miraculous sight they can also spot a movement from high overhead and with unerring accuracy pounce upon a mouse, gopher, or ground squirrel for food.

The eagle and osprey, the greatest of predators, are the most awesome. I saw a bald eagle recently soaring over a river valley not far from my cabin. It looked small way up there, but I knew its enormous wingspread and that it too could spot game from high over the valley—a fish in the river, or possibly carrion close by. I have seen them many times in the Quetico-Superior, found their huge nests of sticks in the tops of old pines, watched their ungainly young being fed; and I have studied the remains of their prey on the whitened ground below. Bald eagles are a gorgeous sight; one never forgets their beauty or the symbol they evoke. There are not too many in this country, except in Alaska, where they are found in uncounted thousands. I think of the McNeil River there at salmon spawning time, when they compete with the brown bear for their leavings. The air over the rapids is alive with their screaming, a high-pitched, ear-penetrating sound different from any other. No other bird dare steal from the eagle except perhaps the osprey. There was an osprey's nest on the Robinson River in the Quetico, with an eagle's nest not far away. The birds played a never-ending game of give and take as the smaller, swifter, and more agile raider would harry its bigger cousin until it dropped its prey.

I do not know the condors of California and the Andes well, as they are far more secretive in their habits and cannot tolerate man. It is a constant battle to protect them as they grow rarer on this continent, though in South America their numbers have not been seriously depleted. The condor is a beautiful bird with its enormous wingspan and black dress; as it rides the updrafts from a mountain valley, drifting high over the peaks of its range, it is a glorious vision of wilderness.

The turkey buzzard is another large predator found over much of the southern part of the continent and in Mexico. The buzzards are supreme scavengers; without them the surface of their territory would be unpleasant to look at. Though there are many scavengers on the ground, it is the vultures that seem to play the important role. In Mexico I have seen them gather together high in the sky the instant an animal is about to die. Black, ugly birds with naked red necks and powerful flesh-tearing beaks, they display a savagery and boldness no other birds possess. A year ago I observed some vultures looking for cattle which had died in the drought of that area. They came down in closer and closer circles and then dropped to the spot where an animal lay; immediately their squawking began as the fight for possession of the carcass took place, a frightening thing to witness.

One seldom sees a buzzard here in the North, but one day near the Canadian border on Crooked Lake I saw six turkey buzzards soaring overhead, low enough to be identified. I wondered why they were in this cold, rocky country, when they belonged far to the south in the land of deserts.

The loggerhead shrike is not usually considered a predator for it actually belongs to the thrush family. However, it looks like a bandit with a black mask through the eyes, and acts like one, too! It doesn't have a song or a scream like many of the other predators, just a sort of whistle, and can dart into a group of birds at a feeder and select one for its food. A small songbird no larger than a robin, it strikes fear when it attacks. I have seen them go in like avenging angels, capture a small bird, and impale it on a thorn. I do not think I am alone in my observation: this diminutive terror has all the instincts of a hawk in its deadly approach.

All predators, large or small, beautiful or ugly, have a role to play in keeping the world free from the stench of death and corruption. They are part of the great cycle of interdependence of all forms of life.

Sounds
of the Night

One evening at my cabin just after dark I was listening to the
moan of the wind through the pines when suddenly it made
one of its frequent pauses, as if resting itself for another onslaught. During this quiet period I heard the rustle of quaking
aspen and birches, softer than that of the pines. I thought of
the whispering of wild rice in the shallow bays and of grassy
meadows.

Not long ago at the cabin during a thunderstorm the sky
was livid with sharp flashes of lightning, and gigantic peals of
thunder rolled and echoed. There was a wild beauty in this
violence, a certain recompense for the Götterdämmerung that
threatened the earth. This tremendous display would have been
exciting in broad daylight, but in the dark it was phenomenal.
When the rain came out of the black clouds, it too sounded
special.

The sound of rapids is more ominous when you cannot see
them, and while listening to their roar you wonder what they

will be like when you have to run them. The same is true of waves beating against the shore and crashing on the rocks. You tell yourself no canoe can be launched in the face of such a sea.

A train whistle at night has a delightful sound for me, full of memories of my boyhood. You hear it in the distance, then it grows louder, and finally fades away into the impenetrable darkness. At times it is almost musical like the old steam locomotives, but even with the modern oil-burning diesels the sound is a deep and abiding pleasure. When on board ship, the moaning of foghorns on a misty night, or the lonely toll of a bell buoy, has the same effect on me.

There is something about animal sounds in the night too. The howling of wolves around Indian villages in the North has a significance only those who live there know and understand. When you are alone in the bush, however, and hear that howl, as wild and blood-curdling as anything can be, primeval reactions surge to the fore and you are filled with ancient forebodings of what is out there in the blackness. A buck close by giving its sharp whistling snort of alarm without warning is startling. All woodsmen know well this strange signal coming out of the deep shadows and take it as a message they have been seen. A beaver slapping its tail with a resounding smack, though you cannot see the splash, shatters the silence when the night is dark and still. A splashing moose sounds like the behemoth it is. Time and again I've lain in my tent and listened, hoping the animal was not in a rut and would not charge the tent or stumble over the tent ropes.

But there are more pleasant sounds. If you are a duck hunter, the whisper of wings overhead is a good omen for the morning. You can almost tell the kind they are by the manner of flight; bluebills are swift with rapid wingbeats, mallards slower and to hear them landing on a pond or lake is music to your ears. Who can ever forget the canvas-tearing sound of a flock coming to rest.

Once on Basswood Lake during late fall I heard a terrible scream like that of a banshee, but having heard it before I knew what it was. I could see a vignette of the winter snows, an owl sinking its talons into a snowshoe hare found playing in the moonlight of an open glade. The only sound that even approaches this screech is the caterwauling of a wildcat, one that sends shivers down your spine.

There is no more irritating sound in a cabin than that of night prowlers, whoever or whatever they might be. One of the most exasperating is that of a deer mouse scurrying around the bunks, over the table, among the dishes, searching for any crumbs left around. You might flash a light, but always too late. Once in a while you catch the beady black eyes of the culprit shining in some out-of-the-way corner to which it has retreated; then the apparition is gone to resume its foray into your larder for the rest of the night.

There is also the occasional bat. You can hear the swish of its wings and a distinct plop as it alights on a screen, where it might hang head down until the dawn. Having heard stories of bats getting tangled in your hair or even using an ear or coat collar for a perch, you crawl under the covers wishing for it to be gone.

Outside the cabin is more trouble, the steady gnaw-gnaw-gnaw of a porcupine chewing on whatever suits its fancy. What it likes best is the handle of an ax or the end of a paddle, both wooden surfaces impregnated with the flavor of sweaty hands. A porcupine can destroy a tool swiftly. You can whittle a new handle from a piece of ash or maple or a paddle from a split length of cedar, but they are poor substitutes for the originals. At night you listen for your enemy, hoping it has had its fill of your possessions.

On one hunting trip I heard a nighttime sound I'd never heard before, one that augured death. Six of us had spent the day hunting several miles away and did not return to our small cabin on the shore of Buck Lake until long after dark. Having fought our way through knee-deep snow in a howling blizzard we were exhausted, wet, and hungry. Jerking open the low door we crowded into a space not more than seven feet square with barely room for us to stand between the stove and the bunks. For a while we rested, out of breath. Then a rifle went off with a shattering roar. In the close confines of that cabin it was something that struck us with horror. Finally someone lit a match, no one saying a word; the flickering light shone on our faces, all six of us. Then an audible sigh of relief and nervous laughter.

"Must have gone through the roof," someone commented; "we're all alive."

By the time we started a fire in the little stove and had supper under way, the tension was gone and everyone relaxed over what could have been a terrible deer-hunting tragedy.

A great tree falling to the ground on a still winter night with the sky full of stars and the silence absolute is something to strike terror in your mind as you stand in the doorway of your cabin. That swoosh is unnerving until you can be sure that it did not fall on your cabin.

You become particularly aware of great danger when, while camped on a mountain slope, you hear an avalanche with its roar of sliding ice, snow, and rocks and wonder if you are in its path. I lost two very good friends, both expert climbers, in such an accident. After it is all over there is nothing to show where you were camped, just a fresh slide. All this goes through your mind when listening to the sounds of the night.

One noise I like at night is that of a harmonica or banjo, for all music is more haunting then, taking on more harmony and appeal than at any other time. That is perhaps why, a century or so ago when wagon trains crossed the Great Plains on their way over the mountains to the Pacific, the musician was treasured by the travelers more than their armed protectors. At night, the wagons were always drawn together in a big circle around a blazing fire; this was the time when the harmonicas and banjos took over. After the heat, dust, and scorching sun, or the freezing cold they had endured, they were ready for music, and, though the musicians may have been amateurs, what came out of their instruments seemed the sweetest sounds the travelers had ever heard. Outside the firelit circle or the glowing tent, all looked back into the darkness from which they had come, listening to the music that spoke of home, loved ones, and friends they had left behind.

Robert W. Service, far to the northwest in the wilds of the Yukon and the northern lights, evoked this when he wrote:

> Do you recollect the bitter Arctic night;
> You camp beside the canyon on the trail;
> Your tent a tiny square of orange light;
> The moon above consumptive like and pale;
> Your supper cooked, your little stove aglow
> You—tired, but snug and happy as a child?
> Then 'twas 'Turkey in the straw' 'till
>   your lips were nearly raw,
> And you hurled your bold defiance at the Wild.

Sounds of the night have magic and mystery.

Wild Encounters

All creatures give character to the land and the terrain from which they came, each one a symbol. None can stand alone, but collectively with all other types they make an environmental pattern in the ecosystem, the ancient game of predatory relationships. How they behave and what they do under stress and in peril is a study in survival.

I remember an incident which illustrates what often happens in the wilds, an encounter that points out not only tragedy, but the concern of a mother for her young. It happened to my son Bob while he was on a guiding trip in the Quetico. His party wanted to see a moose, so he took them to a little bay in the north part of Sarah Lake, a favorite feeding place. They sat quietly in their canoe waiting for the moonrise, listening to the sounds of the dusk: loons calling on the open lake, the twittering of birds, the croaking of frogs, and the loud squawk of a blue heron winging its way toward the open water.

Then they heard a splashing as a cow moose and her ungainly calf left the protection of alder and dwarf birch, wading out toward the middle of the bay. The cow began feeding, immersing her head to grasp lily pad roots. Bob inched the canoe closer until it was within twenty-five feet or so of the animal. The calf stayed in the shallows, apparently afraid to get beyond its depth.

Suddenly from the shore through a stand of willows came a great black bear hurling its way through the muck to the unprotected calf. The cow turned instantly and charged, flailing at the bear with her enormous hooves. The bear retreated to the shore but the cow knew instinctively not to leave the lake. The enemy would simply attack on land, striking down the calf and dragging it away.

Now the bear struck from a different angle and swam toward the beleaguered moose, but the cow whirled and this time struck her assailant. For twenty minutes the battle continued in the water and then suddenly ended. The cow swam to the opposite shore with the calf following close behind. A vignette of death and survival, this time with death thwarted by the courage of a mother defending her own.

We usually think only of larger animals of the land, forgetting that the smaller types are just as indicative of terrain.

I have found lemmings on the tundras all over the world, in the Northwest Territories of Canada, the Yukon, and Alaska, commonplace little creatures living on the seeds and grasses of the Far North. The tales of their migration across rivers and lakes, lemmings plunging recklessly over cliffs only to die in the boiling surf below, are exaggerated, but still persist because there is an element of reality about this kind of story that seems to fascinate the uninformed.

An old friend of mine, Lowell Sumner, told me when we were working together in the Aleutians that no doubt the

migrations were due to stress and overpopulation. As a biologist he knew a great deal about the internal changes that can occur under stress, which may cause lemmings to devour even their own young, attack their neighbors, or move across the tundra to get away from it all. They disperse in the direction of the open sea, rivers, or lakes. Some always stay behind to grow healthy and fat, for with no crowding and unlimited food supplies, they can thrive unchecked until the population builds again.

A great research program is being undertaken on lemming migrations all over the North and in the Scandinavian countries, Siberia, and elsewhere to find out, if possible, why they migrate and more important perhaps to learn if there is some correlation to the problems of our own burgeoning human population with the tensions and stress plaguing us today.

Once when camped on Naknek Lake at the base of the Aleutians off the Alaskan coast, I saw their small, soft gray bodies blending into the moss and grass. Even in daylight one had to be careful, but at night it was impossible, and I remember with horror stepping on one that exploded like a balloon. They were well fed there so it must have been something other than food that drove them on. Foxes, bears, wolverines, ravens, and eagles followed them, for here was a feast for the taking. I think of the Far North as lemming country. Because of them the Arctic has an unusual ecological quality of its own.

The pine marten of the North and Northwest is a member of the weasel family which feeds on squirrels and birds in the high branches of the pines. This animal is associated in my mind with the old primeval forests because it thrives only in tall coniferous timber.

One day at the Point three baby mink played at the end of the dock, totally unafraid. When they slipped into the water

I knew the mother was near. Later I found their droppings on the swimming dock near the sauna, where they had been feeding on crayfish, clams, and frogs.

Animals do give character to the land. No matter how insignificant any species may appear to be, it contributes to the ecological pyramid, and if we look at all of them with understanding eyes we will know this to be true.

The Prairies

The prairies of this country, with their tremendous beauty and historical significance, are found throughout Illinois and in the Red River Valley of northwestern Minnesota. Their greatest expanse is in the West, where they once covered thousands of square miles. For many centuries prairie grasses have grown, each year laying a deposit of humus until the soil beneath was rich and black, more so than any other on the continent. Because of their great fertility, these soils produce immense quantities of grain. It is not surprising these global areas provide enough food to have earned them the coveted title Bread-basket of the World.

However, these lands could not continue as prairies without the fires set by Indians or through natural causes such as lightning. Without periodic burning the grasslands would grow up to weeds and brush and eventually to trees.

The name "prairie" crops up everywhere—Prairie du Chien, a small town in the central part of Wisconsin, Prairie

Portage in Minnesota, and Prairie River east of the Twin Cities of St. Paul and Minneapolis, Minnesota. People who live on these prairies are marked by them; unlike forest dwellers hemmed in by trees, they need open space and unlimited horizons, sunsets, moonrises, and shooting stars. The colorful display of asters and sunflowers and the waving grasses are like an open sea billowing and rolling along in the wake of the unending winds.

There are two types of prairie grasses: the short grass, not much more than three or four feet; and the tall, which stands higher than a man or horse, making it not unusual in the early days for riders to get lost forcing their way through it. The prairies produced huge numbers of buffalo, elk, and antelope. Native tribes lived on them for centuries until the white man's guns killed most of their food. There were herds extending for miles, as far as the eye could see. Early artists depicted them crossing the wide Missouri River or such tributaries as the River Platte. There were buffalo jumps where Indians forced them over jagged cliffs, and one where even today you can find whitened skulls with the horns still intact deep among the talus below the cliffs. On my last trip I visited a site in Montana and my imagination ran rampant. I could see young Indians riding bareback with whoops and cries forcing the buffalo over the edge; women butchering the carcasses, cutting out the prized tongues, the big fat humps, and the livers. They were happy knowing their families would feast well for days.

The buffalo was an important part of the prairie Indian economy but it was the horse that gave the Indians mobility, enabling them to ride everywhere. Until the horse all hunting was done on foot—a dangerous practice, for the hunters were vulnerable to stampeding herds and could be trampled to death if caught in the path of their pounding hooves.

The Indians prayed to their Great Spirit to give them buffalo when they were in need. Their tall conical tepees made of sewn buffalo hides, creamy white in color, were decorated with paintings of buffalo and the totems of great hunters and warriors who had distinguished themselves. I know a Chippewa chief, named Crazy Horse in tribute to the horses inherited from the Spaniards, who called his son Little Buffalo.

But all this is of the past when prairies seemed limitless, and the time has now come to save the last pitiful remnants from the ravages of the plow and dust storms that began when settlers broke the thick primeval sod of tough matted roots. They used four-horse teams and immense breaking plows to turn over the black soil, exposing it to winds and rains. I saw one of these storms in western Minnesota, watched the unrelenting winds pile up dust along the fencerows, engulfing homes, pastures and cropland, farm machinery, and burying the hopeful dreams of people living out their lives on the rich farms they had worked so faithfully. Now there was no choice but to abandon them forever. All this happened during the depression of the 1930's, not only in Minnesota, but also on the prairies of Nebraska, Kansas, and neighboring states. With the need for more grain to feed a hungry and desperate world faced with drought and famine, the cycle was being repeated.

In recent years the Nature Conservancy has made efforts to purchase areas of prairie in Minnesota, and the tall grass of Kansas. A friend of mine, Newell Searle, working with this organization, concentrated on small remnants of the old prairies that had not been disturbed, such as railroad rights of way, old cemeteries, the edges of pastures, and even hidden corners close to the large cities. After fencing off selected plots, they set controlled fires to bring back the grasses and flowers that grew with them. Botany and ecology professors from universities and colleges took their students on field trips to observe the results.

The Aldo Leopold Wild Life Refuge in southern Wisconsin near Madison, established by the man who wrote *A Sand County Almanac,* is an example of what can be done to bring the prairie back to its original state. The people of Madison had become very fond of the area just a few miles north of the city, and when the ecologists were ready to burn the region, everyone was aghast at the monstrosity of the idea. No one could do this to their refuge without reckoning with them! An educational campaign was conducted during the winter months which explained scientifically why the program was necessary. In the spring when the residents watched the perimeter of burning grass, it was with understanding; later there was even delight when flowers emerged again in profusion.

El Coyote

I awakened the other morning just before dawn and heard the coyotes singing their beautiful song. As the short yipping barks increased, they became a stirring crescendo. First there was only one, then two or three, until it seemed as though there were a dozen. Coyotes always choose special places such as high hills or promontories for their concerts to greet a sun- or moonrise. This music might have a definite purpose in greeting others of their kind, but I feel they sing because they like to hear the sound of their own voices.

Many who have heard it call the coyote the "song dog of the West"; Indians called it "the wonder dog." As Ernest Thompson Seton once said, "I wish I could do justice to your spirit. Your voice thrills us in a song that is the very nature of all songs of joy and gladness." It would be a sad day if ever one camped in the open sagebrush flats without hearing the coyote sing of peace and wilderness.

What sort of creature is *Canis latrans*? What is he called in

Mexico, all over the West, and now in this area? He is known in Spanish as *coyote*, the name given this wild dog by the Spaniards when they first came to the Southwest five hundred years ago. A small animal about two feet ten inches tall and weighing between seventeen and twenty-six pounds, the coyote is a sort of grizzled, brownish-gray color but has no great ruff over the shoulders like the much larger wolf. There are a dozen subspecies of this animal called "troubador of the desert," this Ishmaelite living by its wits.

Its range is from lower Mexico to the Great Lakes, west to the Pacific Coast, and northwest as far as Great Slave Lake. There were three million of them in primitive times, but they have decreased greatly since modern man began his campaign of shooting, poisoning, and trapping. In spite of all, the coyote has been able to survive through sheer cunning and intelligence. This animal is now found as far north as the Yukon and Alaska, within a hundred miles of the Arctic Ocean.

The coyote has infiltrated the domain of the wolf and is now found in northeastern Minnesota as far as Duluth and beyond, where I have heard it sing outside my window. Of all wild animals, this one seems best to have solved the riddle of life; it will no doubt be with us forever.

Like most of the wolf family the coyote is monogamous; the male helps to feed and care for the young and protects the den. The mating period is during the last two weeks in February, and the young are born in the latter half of April.

When the pups are about to arrive, the female begins to look for a denning site, a sandy bank preferably, with a southern exposure so the pups can roll and play in the sunlight. Sometimes she will move into an existing burrow such as a fox or badger hole. The den is a rather complicated affair, often several feet underground running horizontal to the surface,

with an air hole for ventilation and separate rooms for storing food, resting, and sleeping. The coyotes provide themselves with but a single entrance, unlike other burrowers, who usually have an escape hatch in case the entrance is invaded by an enemy. The nesting chamber is about three feet in diameter, lined with grass or fur, but members of the family may require sleeping places of their own—one for the pups, a large and elaborate one for the mother and her young, and even a private one for the male, a sort of bachelor quarters where he could escape the racket of barking and playing pups.

At six weeks the pups start to play, and by July they are half-grown and begin to heed the cry of the mother. By October they are full-grown and almost on their own, but the mother still disgorges food for them when they are unsuccessful in their own foraging. With one litter a season, not breeding until the second year, and a lifespan of ten to twelve years, the coyote lives a short, precarious life.

As the pups begin to mature they will venture out to sit in front of the den to await the return of the mother with their food. Would-be intruders are lured by her into old abandoned dens. Socially the coyotes are a very closely knit family with elaborate rituals governing their affairs.

The coyote is an excellent hunter, employing strategy and subterfuge to a remarkable extent. While its food may be almost anything that flies, walks, swims, or burrows in the earth (such as insects, worms, ants, salamanders, and mice), the coyote's major prey is larger animals. In stalking prairie dogs it will walk close to a hole and then past it, hoping the victim will surface to scream its defiance and hatred at the hunter. The hunter, hiding near, will then spring on the unsuspecting rodent and capture it.

Coyotes also use a relay type of hunting, with a second

animal taking up the chase to relieve the first when it has tired. This relay may work with more than two until the poor exhausted prey lies down and waits for fate to take its course. This can happen in the northern woods as well as on the western prairies and applies to game both large and small— jackrabbits, antelopes, and deer. It may seem as though the coyote is a killer at heart, but actually it is often the rancher's or farmer's best friend as it eliminates creatures that might be pests. Once in a while it might steal a sheep or raid the chicken coop or harass a newborn calf, but by and large the coyote is beneficial in many ways, occupying a valuable niche in the overall ecology of its region.

The coyote can reach tremendous speeds—up to seventy miles per hour—and can outdistance most pursuers. This animal stores its food much like the wolf does, burying a kill to return for it later. Knowing this trait, trappers will poison the carcasses; however, the coyote, being wary, often does not return.

Perhaps it would be interesting to end this chapter with an account of how Indians used to hunt coyotes with a bow and arrow, in the old way. They respected the coyote, for it was part of their legendary and religious beliefs. One who killed a coyote had to ask its permission, and would only do so if it were needed for food or raiment. They felt such wise and clever creatures deserved a more dignified demise than those dealt by poison, traps, or guns. I found this account in an Ernest Thompson Seton book, as told by a half-breed Indian guide to a white companion eighty years ago.

We built a blind high enough so we could hide behind it, then carried brush to scatter around as a camouflage. By the time we had finished, darkness began to gather.

Then far across the valley a coyote sounded. In an instant many had gathered from all around. When the coyote barked, the Indian answered. Each time the coyote's cry came back out of the shadows, it was much nearer. The Indian turned on his side and barked twice, short and sharp unlike the first. Then almost before the sound left his lips, he lifted his voice in the long howl which is the mark of the coyote tribe all over the West.

This time the call from the animal was much closer. Then a shadow slipped across the moonlit patch of ground. Again my companion called seductively and then lay still, the last echoes dying in his throat. The coyote was deceived and came out in plain sight, close to the blind. I tried to raise my rifle but the Indian laid his hand on mine. Then I saw the white of his bow and heard the swish of the arrow. The little wolf leaped into the air and fell back dead.

This has been the story of the coyote famed and loved for its desert song. No matter how settled the land, fenced and cut up by farms, towns, and cities, chances are that a hundred or a thousand years from now the coyote will flourish as before. Here is a toast to El Coyote the invincible; may he always make music in the dusk and the dawning.

Hummingbird Rapids

One bright midsummer's day Elizabeth and I were on a canoe trip along the old Dawson Trail in Canada with a famous historian of the fur trade, Grace Lee Nute. We were on the Maligne River, so named by the French, meaning bad and dangerous, with several rapids to run; Elizabeth was sitting in the center and Grace in the bow. In the middle of the rapids we noticed that a hummingbird was attracted to Elizabeth's red cap, making constant passes at it. We were so engrossed with the tiny bird's antics we momentarily forgot about the rapids until the canoe swung broadside and we were in danger of swamping. I jumped into the water, which was waist deep, turned the canoe, and guided it to the shore to empty out the sloshing wetness. No harm done, just a little unwarranted excitement. We decided to call the place Hummingbird Rapids.

Many places have delightful names: the Kawishiwi, Ogish-gemuncie, and Saganaga; the poet lakes on the Canadian side of the border, Shelley and Keats; Yum-Yum, from a Broadway production; Chatterton, named by someone who no doubt had read romantic poems by the eighteenth-century poet Thomas Chatterton. Whoever paddled through this area must have been in a poetic frame of mind, thinking of things he had read and seen.

There are also names on both sides of the border that indicate no particular imagination, just boredom with bodies of water or rivers some early explorer or surveyor had given no designation at all. One string of lovely lakes on the Quetico side of the border has been called This Man's, That Man's, No Man's, and the Other Man's lake. To match it on the American side, in the Superior National Forest are Lake One, Lake Two, Lake Three, and Lake Four, which are shown on aerial maps, geodetic surveys, as well as in the history of the region.

On Artillery Lake in the spring you can hear the booming of the ice as it begins to break up, bashing against the shores —or could it have been only thunder during a summer shower? I like the French names: Grand Marais and Little Marais, meaning a swampy bay, Lac des Mille Lacs, lake of a thousand smaller lakes. La Chine has great appeal, a name given to a rapids on the Ottawa River in Ontario by early explorers who believed they were en route to China and the Orient, which lay beyond the Northwest Passage that had lured them on for two centuries. Deux Rivières, place of two rivers, was a route I knew well in my guiding days. Curtain Falls—Le Rideau—was a dramatic and pretty place where many early travelers stopped. Rainy River on the international border was another, known as Rivière l'Pluie.

Near Grand Portage is Cherry Portage Petit Vaseaux, and at the upper end of Lake of the Woods, Rat Portage, or Portage la Marte. White Wood Portage, or Prairie Portage, was once known as Portage des Bois Blanc because of the birches growing there. Now this place is known as Basswood Lake, with Basswood River its outlet, named because the English of the Northwest Company could not pronounce Portage des Bois Blanc. The only white wood they knew was the linden, or basswood of England and Europe, so they named it Basswood, a name it proudly bears to this day.

This chapter would not be complete without mention of La Parisian Rapids, in Ontario, where artifacts of the fur trade were found in abundance—kettles, knives, trade axes, flint and steel, beads and traps, and, most important, the muskets so valuable to the Indians who were supplying the fur. It is ironic that when they went to war against the white man, the Indians turned the muskets, leaden balls, and powder against him and his practice of robbing and destroying the culture of their people.

I often think of Hummingbird Rapids and the names of many lakes and rivers known long ago—the French names, especially, which have the same delightful appeal as the chansons voyageurs sang as they traversed these waters. Names are important, for they carry a message, and those who do not know what they mean are missing the joy of intimacy with them.

Arrowheads

When I first came to Listening Point I searched for arrowheads in the clean sand of the beach. Knowing that Indians used to camp there, I was not surprised to find several beautifully made ones. They were not of flint, which is scarce in this area, but of yellowish-brown chert and reddish-colored jasper. I have always hunted these treasures, for they are a link with the past and speak of bygone eras.

I have found arrowheads in the Far West made of black volcanic obsidian below the talused cliffs of Wyoming and Montana. The arrowheads were so valuable that specimens of the rock were traded with other tribes, who paid handsomely for them with whatever they could give of their own substance.

Recently I was at the excavation of an elephant kill site on the Lehner ranch of the San Pedro Valley near Hereford, Arizona. I was a guest of Ed Lehner and was accompanied by Emil Haury, famous archeologist and anthropologist. In

1955–56, my hosts told me, the Arizona State Museum had excavated an elephant kill site and found several projectiles and butchering tools and some hearth charcoal among the remains of nine immature mammoths and elements of horse, bison, and tapir. Bones and artifacts were found in the gravel of a former stream and exposed in an eroded bank.

It was fascinating to go over the ancient stream bed, see the eroding banks, and picture what had taken place there thousands of years ago. I felt as if I were a member of a hunting team. My hosts showed me where the bones were located and I actually found a few fragments, which I tucked into my pocket as a reminder. I was impressed with what archeologists call a dig and the extreme care with which everything is retrieved.

It was a wonderful experience to have been a small part of an expedition into the past, one that gave me a different perspective and a long leap backward. Never again would I pick up an arrowhead without thinking of my experience in Arizona. The entire process of learning to shape tools marks the transition between primitive man and his emergence into a maker of hunting implements that eventually led into the machine age of our Western civilization.

That first discovery of mine at Listening Point was far more important than I realized, for it opened a door into a realm I had never fully understood, one that covered remote stretches of this continent and others. I once met L. S. B. Leakey of Africa and listened to him tell of his lifelong search for evidence of primitive man in an eroded canyon of the old Olduvai. What gave him clues was finding rudely made artifacts which indicated early human progress. He found skeletal remains that, to the astonishment of the scientific world, extended the life of *Homo sapiens* several million years. His work is being continued by his widow and son, who are as dedicated as he was.

On an expedition in the Aleutian chain of Alaska, I campcd at the site of another dig. Huge mammoth bones had been unearthed, but there had been no careful excavations such as were done in Arizona, just a happenstance finding of enormous tusks in the muck of a river. They were discolored and brown ("antique ivory," they call it in the trade), and much prized for carving into jewelry and other purposes. Dr. Haury has done considerable research along the Alaskan coast off Nome and the Onion River and has found implements as intcrcsting as those in his beloved Arizona. The search goes on in many parts of the world, certainly far removed from where it all started for me on Listening Point in the sand of an old Indian campground.

Rock Hound

I am surrounded by rocks. Each one reminds me of some place I have been, and whenever I come back from an expedition my pack is heavy. Beside me as I write is a beautiful flat rock rounded by the waves of some lake in the Far North, and impressed on one side is a perfect willow leaf.

Another of my very special specimens is one I ran across while on a pack trip in the Big Horn mountains of Wyoming. Always on the lookout, even when riding a horse along a mountain trail, I noticed a rather strange stone my mount had kicked while scrambling for a foothold. Dismounting, I retrieved it though it was cracked. As I pulled it apart several fossil imprints were exposed: one like a sand dollar, another a cluster of tiny flat marks, possibly limpets, the third like a snail shell. What a marvelous find, and all because my horse nearly stumbled. Whenever I look at the stone, that western trip comes vividly to mind.

On the east coast of Hudson Bay I discovered some ripple

marks on a bed of quartzite, an unmistakable sign of tidal waves of an ancient sea. Just how it was formed is difficult to explain. I brought back a similar specimen from the south of England. I call it my fossil raindrop, as it really must have been formed during a pelting rainstorm that left large imprints in the soft mud. After being exposed it was covered with dust blown over it by the wind, and then submerged again and subjected to the same treatment, preserving those raindrops for me to see.

Not far from where I found the raindrops I gathered a strange-looking cluster of stems from a prehistoric cycad. The vertical striations are very plain and speak of a forgotten time when there were mud flats where the plant grew tall and was at last uncovered.

I also have a small greenish stone found at the eastern end of Great Bear Lake south of the Arctic Ocean. Geologists flying over this region noticed a colored glow through the shallow water and called it cobalt bloom. This is the hue that betrayed vast deposits of uranium which, during the last days of the Second World War, was used to make the nuclear bombs that leveled Nagasaki and Hiroshima, killing many thousands of people and disfiguring many more, a sad message from the greenish specimen on my desk.

There are many others, each having a story to tell. One is a block of garnet embedded in a black mixture of feldspar, biotite, and other minerals. I uncovered it in New Hampshire, where garnet is abundant, and recall a roadway surfaced with crushed crystals that glistened when a car drove over them at night. Garnet is a deep, reddish purple, and, to people aware of its beauty, it is a precious stone.

I once discovered a sample of quartz at an old abandoned mine worked during a gold strike a century ago. There was not enough gold there to mine, and like many such strikes all over the world, nothing is left but tunnels and shafts, broken-down cabins, and dreams lost and forgotten. My bit of quartz is interlaced with the blackish tint of silver and tiny specks of gold, the royal metal which started many a gold rush and hope of fortunes that never materialized.

In the stone wall which bounds my home are further trea-sures gathered mostly in my own surroundings, and some from Alaska. There are several pieces of reddish jasper, some inter-laced with hematite. I recall roaming the woods a few miles south of my home and finding a chunk of jasper weighing ten to twelve pounds in a glacial rock pile. Perhaps there for thousands of years, it simply shone in the sunlight. It is now in my stone wall, where I can admire it.

Beside it is a rock of pillow lava, so called because the gases during a volcanic period bubbled through the molten mass forcing their way through. Another of my prizes is a very heavy rock, the iron core of a fumarole escape duct which may have been transported thousands of miles or could have origi-nated in this area. It shows how the gases first formed in a tiny aperture and then as they crystallized the opening grew, ring by ring, much like rings in a tree. It was interesting as I examined it to find some areas of jasper, the same I prized so highly: an affiliation, it seems, wherever there is great heat from a subterranean source.

The Aleutian chain of Alaska known as the Valley of Ten Thousand Smokes is in Katmai National Monument. After spending some time there studying the fumaroles, I learned that if one smoking vent was closed, the escaping gases could come out at another, proof the formation was honeycombed with channels. I flew over it one day when fumes and smoke, as they poured out of the crater, made visibility almost zero.

Camped one night on the shore of a little lake, I found bits of pumice floating off the beach. The sample I have is somewhat orange, full of gaseous vesicles, or cavities in the rock formed by the gases. Some of the valley has ridges of this material, scored by the erosion of heavy rains and winds. In 1912, when Katmai blew its top and cinders were scattered over a large area, there was much damage and no doubt loss of life. But the area has recovered as I could tell by my small piece of pumice.

On the wall is an odd-looking conglomerate from the Charley River in the eastern part of Alaska. Sig Jr. found it on a canoe trip and also brought me a handful of beautiful agates tumbled in the rapids of the river. They range from yellow to amber, shining in the light. As I study the concentric rings of their creation, this variegated chalcedony with its crystallized clouds and stripes originating from the central core, I understand why it is so appealing.

Glacial Clay

Five miles north of my home is a little lake called Bass Lake. I always found it to be an interesting body of water and traveled it frequently on my way to the Range River and Jackfish Bay of Basswood Lake and down the old voyageur route along the border. Bass was connected with Low Lake to the east and reached by a portage over a steep moraine.

One night in late April I was camped at its upper end intending to take the old route to the north in the morning. During the night I heard a tremendous roar and wondered if a storm were approaching, but the tent was near the end of the portage on high ground so I wasn't worried. The roar was followed by a lower sound as though there were water running. Finally I fell asleep, although puzzled and apprehensive.

The next morning I walked down to the landing beside a log, which was helpful in loading the canoe, and I literally froze in amazement. The water was gone and down below was only a stretch of sandy bottom! I walked out gingerly, for there might be sinkholes in mucky places, and then began to hike to the bottom of old Bass Lake. In the far end where the esker used to be was a great opening. Then I looked up at the old shorelines and could see that the water had dropped about forty feet, leaving the little islands halfway down the lake high and dry. One of them had a cedar shore and showed the browse line the deer had made during the past winters, now ridiculously far above the present water level. I thought of the animals that had made those islands their home, the mink, the muskrat, the great blue heron that stood in the shallows at one end; they would all have to seek new shelters.

How and why had this happened? There had to be a cause, and I was determined to find it out. I remembered in logging days there was a sluiceway through a ditch at the top of the moraine to carry the logs from Bass to Low Lake below. From there they were rafted to the railroad nearby in Winton, Minnesota, and the mills on Fall Lake.

When I reached Low, I realized I was walking through the stickiest lacustrine blue clay I had ever experienced. Then I understood! The sluiceway ditch had broken the ancient seal which had kept the moraine intact for ten thousand years. The water had seeped down through the sand and lubricated the clay on which it rested, and cutting the pine had played its part in the erosion. When the spring flood period came, the huge deposit of sand and boulders merely slipped away on the greasy surface underneath. It was as simple as that.

I have run into such places in other areas, once on a canoe trip in the north of Canada when I made the mistake of stepping out of the canoe in preparing to line it down a rapids. I'll never forget how the clay held on to my boots so firmly it was almost impossible to get my feet out. The canoe carried the blue clay for days.

I was in Anchorage, Alaska, in 1964, shortly after an earthquake had practically leveled the business district of the town. It was frightening to see the devastation, but the worst was in a suburb overlooking Turnagain Arm where a terrible thing occurred. Homes overlooking the beautiful bay began sliding out on the blue clay underlying the area, the same kind responsible for the disaster on Bass Lake. Some lives were lost, and, in the middle of the night, people caught in the movement landed in piles of broken rubble and tangled debris on the beach several hundred yards below. I marveled later at how few were killed.

Now people in Anchorage are moving back to the place they once called home, building a little farther back than they first did, all this in spite of the warnings of geologists and seismologists. When asked why, one of the builders who was going ahead with his plans said scornfully: "These experts from Washington don't know what they're talking about." Here was the same kind of thinking as that of people who rebuild on the flood plains of rivers.

Later, after the changing of Bass and Low Lakes, I took a canoe trip from the border up the Range River route just to see what the flood had done. I shall never forget the sight of the piles of logs and mud on either side of the river. At times it was very difficult to surmount the obstacles. Grass, brush, and debris marked the high point of the flood that had surged through the river and straightened its course, cutting across the bends. It would have been disastrous to have been on the river when the high waters came barreling through.

I know what the blue clay means to an old friend of mine, a potter who swears there is no finer clay in the world than found on the portage between Bass and Low. I have several of his bowls, one decorated with Indian paintings, blue showing through a highly polished brown glaze.

Ripple Marks

One beautiful day in late October I was enjoying the blue and golden plumes of tamaracks along the roadside, which stood like sentinels in every bog. Though most of the color was gone, patches of large-toothed aspen had turned to peach in protected places where the wind had not touched them, birches were purple at their tips, and blueberries were bright red against the ground. This was the time of year called Indian summer in the North and it was exciting to see the last bright displays before the coming gales and snows would tear the foliage from the trees. What a pity, I thought, to miss a minute of all this.

I had been invited by my friend Jack B. Malcolm to go underground to see the Minnamax Exploration Project of which he was in charge. I had accepted with alacrity, partly because of my own geological background and also because Malcolm was a geologist with worldwide experience in his field. I knew large deposits of copper and nickel lay under the famous Duluth gabbro (rock composed of labradorite), a great arc slicing through the Boundary Waters Canoe Area down to Lake Superior. These deposits had never been thoroughly explored before although their presence would affect the land of the voyageurs, its lakes, rivers, and forests, known until now only for its beauty, historical significance, and recreational value.

The mine was about twenty miles south of my home, and as Jack explained it was an experimental shaft seventeen hundred feet deep with stopes and drifts radiating out from its lowest level. We studied maps and profiles of the formation, and his staff made clear what the various formations meant as far as actual mining was involved. It was also explained where veins of copper nickel lay, and I was shown drill cores made at various levels of depth—nearly five million dollars' worth, an investment of seven years of drilling, the real record of the ore body.

Long ago I had gone underground in the mine in Soudan, Minnesota, on the Vermilion Range nearby, one of the richest iron deposits ever found, a mine that was later closed when the ore played out. The miners had old-fashioned acetylene lights fastened to their hard hats while working the drifts. They were mining the green rock associated with the beds of ore but there were always some veins of native copper. The enormous crystals of quartz and gold bearing intrusions had impressed me most, but it was in search of gold that prospectors found the iron.

I knew something of what going down into the bowels of the earth meant, but I was exhilarated because I was to look at an area of mineralization I had never seen before. Minnamax was a pilot plant, exploring the possibilities of a copper nickel deposit.

Before we descended I met two young biologists who had been on the team for three years, monitoring the impact of seepage and drainage from the exposed materials brought to the surface. They showed me the herbarium they had put together—almost a hundred and fifty specimens collected during this time, to be used as an aid in finding out how vegetation might be affected and environmental damage assessed before any operation began.

When it was time to go down, Jack Malcolm, two other geologists, and I were fitted with rubber suits, waterproof boots, a battery light, and all the necessary paraphernalia. We stepped into the lift, the door clanked shut, and we began to descend. Water was dripping everywhere—500 feet . . . 1000 . . . 1500—and we went slowly so we could see the sides of the shaft. At last a bright light, and we were on the lowest level, where I found myself in a different world. Seeing the mine through the geologists' eyes brought back my own training, though it had been much different from theirs. Geology in my youth was a rather primitive science; we used old textbooks which, while generally accurate, contained data that were a far cry from modern knowledge of the earth's crust.

Nevertheless old terms came back to me as I heard talk of faults and fractures, slickensides, dips, and strike intrusions into bedrocks and green-stone such as the veins of the Knife Lake slates which I had studied long ago and seen at the surface. Tilted at a steep angle they showed the ripple marks in formations laid down in the mud and silt of ancient seas. On a trip to Knife Lake several years before, I had packed some excellent flat specimens across many portages. They were greenish in color, tortured and twisted under the stress of volcanic pressures. I laid some in a walk from my study to the house, and others near my cabin. When washed by the rain they glitter.

And now in the mine, almost two thousand feet below the surface, I was seeing them again, old friends of early days.

The Lake Superior gabbro was the rock of the north shore of the big lake. Hard and unyielding, it has withstood the elements for millions of years. This was the formation that had produced the great ore deposits of the Mesabi and Vermilion ranges, a veritable cross-section of the dynamism of the shifting earth's crust that made the land what it is.

We worked our way down a long stope, wading through puddles at times dangerously deep, keeping a hand on the wall to steady ourselves. Our lights played on veins of ore, making them glow. Before me is a sample of that trip, in which the greenish tinge of copper sulfide speaks of richness, and with it a very special sample of bornite, greenish blue—a gift of one of the geologists. It runs very high in copper nickel content, indicative of what ore an operating mine could depend on.

"Some day," said Jack, "this might be worth mining. Pay dirt, we call it. If there is enough it could be worth billions."

"But what about the impact of this mining on the environment?" I asked. "What will big mines mean to this beautiful country if a smelter is built to process and refine the ore?"

"You've got to swim with the tide," he replied; "all over the world there is a revolution in thinking. No longer does industry call the tune. For the first time in history care of the environment is of paramount importance. It's a matter of human survival. There's no use fighting the trend, for if you do you're on a losing team."

With that I was content, for no one knew the score at the moment. Nor could anyone foretell the desperate need of our civilization for copper nickel and other minerals if we were to progress and continue to enjoy the standard of living we have learned to take for granted.

"Development could come when the time is ripe," he continued, "when we know at last how to mine and refine our product without destroying our base, which in the last analysis is the environment itself."

We had talked about millennia and geological vistas going back seven billion years. Few on the surface could comprehend what I had seen this memorable day. My mind was literally exploding with ideas, questions of energy, geothermal power, the economic crisis.

When it was over we trudged back to the bright lights of the cage area, the doors clanged again, and we began the dripping ride to the top. Suddenly we were in the bright sunshine and I looked around me in wonder. The tamaracks were still gold and the roadsides flecked with color just as I left them a few hours before. What I had seen and heard boded well for the future. No one could predict the end, but with growing knowledge and understanding, things would work out. And how could one be pessimistic on such a beautiful fall day!

Sand Dunes

Sand dunes are strange, wonderful, fascinating places that change continually. They are children of the wind, geologically formed from the erosion of the land, and are found all over the world—in the vast Sahara, on the coasts of this continent, in the Midwest and Southwest.

Cape Cod National Seashore, where the pilgrims landed three hundred years ago, besides having a great historical significance possesses magnificent dunes. As one watches the white foaming surf washing against the shores of the Atlantic Coast and hears the wind whistling over the high dunes it looks like a place where men could not exist for long.

Cape Hatteras, off the east coast of North Carolina, has the same type of shore but is considered far more dangerous, for countless ships have floundered on its shoals, and wrecks lie everywhere beaten into whitened broken hulks by the waves. Walking along that beach one ponders the power of the sea and how many lives have been lost, with dreams ended there forever.

The Oregon dunes shaped by waves of the broad Pacific are different. Invaded by the living dunes, the old ones stand sere, bleached, and broken in the teeth of the wind; the new ones are still green and growing, but they too will die some day, as is their fate. Beach grass lives for a time and the circular tracery of a tuft on the sand is a work of art. Eventually the grass can no longer hold on, and the march of dunes continues inland.

Strange as it may seem, dunes are found in Colorado and the Southwest. But how, you ask, can they be so far away from the ocean? The answer is that the region was once the bottom of an ancient sea whose shores covered vast expanses inland. As the waters receded and the land rose, the winds broke the old headlands and ledges into a crystalline white or reddish sand, depending on the formation.

The White Sands National Monument in the San Andreas Mountains of New Mexico has desert plants, yucca, sumacs, and sometimes cottonwoods. They fight to keep their heads above the huge rolling waves of crystalline sands derived from gypsum (the world's largest deposit), and there are dunes there up to fifty feet in height. Under the blistering heat of the sun, gypsum bakes into plaster of Paris, which makes these shimmering white dunes appear like giant snowdrifts in the desert.

The Great Sand Dunes National Monument lying south of the Rocky Mountains, and below the Santo de Christo Range, as well as El Morro National Monument of western New Mexico, has a similar geological history. Seven thousand years ago northeastern New Mexico shook with volcanic eruptions forming huge cinder cones. High winds in this area drive the volcanic sand through the fourteen-thousand-foot range of mountains and passes, piling dunes seven hundred feet high.

Sand Dunes

In northern Colorado where the desert meets the mountain, the winds are just as destructive. From the southwest across the heat-hazed expanse of the San Luis Valley they push the loose sand and, as the velocity lessens, drop their burdens at the mountain's base. After many centuries sand dunes have smothered fifty square miles with crests above the valley floor, the loftiest dunes of the inland states.

The Lake Michigan dunes are entirely different, not the result of volcanic eruptions but formed by gales sweeping down several hundred miles from the north. Set aside as the Michigan Dunes National Lake Shore, it is now a preserved dune area. I walked the beach at the southern end of the lake, watching the rollers coming down. It was dusk, and I could see the glittering lights of the city of Chicago and the smoking mills of Gary, Indiana, below. I thought how wonderful it was to have these dunes serve as a wilderness to this huge metropolis, with their bogs, ponds, and sluggish streams. Years ago I made an ecological study of this area, and like others who came I was entranced with its wild exotic beauty and plants found nowhere else in the Far North.

The Lake Superior dunes were formed from a great postglacial sea that once covered all the lake and beyond to the north. The winds piled the sands of erosion over much of northwestern Wisconsin. Today the dunes are covered with jackpine and scrub oak bleached white, and broken, almost completely hidden by sand. New ones trying to grow are struggling to survive. Settlers came here and found the land easy to clear, with no problem in cutting the small trees or grubbing out stumps from the sandy soil. Others called these invaders "jackpine savages" who did not realize the land was worthless for farming. As a result of the soil's poor quality, the North Country is littered with decaying, tumbled down cabins overgrown with weeds and brush, evidence of a once-glowing hope of carving new homes in the wilderness.

Dunes are children of the wind and meant much to men who chose to live on their shifting sands. They are beautiful it is true, but this is not enough for survival.

Waiting

Toward the end of March when the ground is still covered with ice and snow and the temperatures dip to fifty below, one goes into a sort of trance. Everyone watches weather reports over the area, almost gloating to hear that somewhere else gales are worse than one's own. Then comes a day when the sun bursts out of the overcast and everyone stands, even for a brief moment, to bask in its warmth. It is miraculous, cannot be true, but it has happened; and as though to prove it, the chickadees, warmed for the first time in months, sing their plaintive mating song.

There are often times of waiting, as when, especially on expeditions, one looks for a squally storm to end after the discomfort of days when waves were high and rain was constant. One cannot move on, the surf making it impossible to launch the canoes. All anyone can do is gather firewood, always soggy and wet, stay close to a smoky fire discussing the chance of getting a break from the monotony, and when conversation lags stare into the flames. If the weather does not change for days, food and clothing get moldy and one prays for a warm wind so things can be hung out to dry and the food laid on a tarp.

Even in clear weather one often cannot travel during the day because of waves that are too rough, and it is necessary to wait until evening when the wind dies down. Learn to travel at night is a bonanza in itself. The stars can be used as a guide, and one can watch the display of northern lights and listen to sounds missed during the day, the hooting of owls or calling of wolves. Once on a cloudy night with no stars, we were lost on the Churchill River. Trying without success to navigate by the feel of the water, we were wary of the rapids ahead. A pair of mallards appeared above and, knowing they would not leave the river but would fly down its course, we gratefully followed them and soon came to a very nice campsite.

At the end of a trip in the Far North one usually expects a launch tow at the end of a big lake, or the pick-up flight. I have listened anxiously for the drone of a motor, and when it doesn't come spirits and tempers get short. Could I have made a mistake in the time or day? One paces up and down, watches the sky or water, and if nothing is seen goes back to the fire for another cup of tea. Sometimes the plane is several days late, the pilot thwarted in his arrival perhaps by having a forest fire to patrol, a sick Indian to bring out, or mechanical trouble. The launch driver may have been waiting to take another party to a different spot than ours, meaning a long detour. If a day goes by, or even two, one just makes the best of it, fishing if the weather is good, cooking up the last reserve of food, hoping there is enough to last.

And then the launch arrives, or the plane comes in over the horizon, the pontoons touch the shore, the canoe is tied on and the packs and outfit thrown in. The long wait is over.

On a trip in the Quetico on Argo Lake, we suffered through three long, miserable days, too rainy to fish or do anything but try to keep dry, until on the afternoon of the third the gray clouds parted and the sun emerged! We were camped near a good trout hole, my son Sig Jr., his cousin Curt, and I. We decided to catch our dinner, and Curt sat in the middle of the canoe with the rod and a big copper spoon. Almost immediately he had a strike, no ordinary one for it bore down into the depths and made powerful runs, all but stripping the line off the reel, so close it might have torn the rod from Curt's hands. Finally after forty-five minutes the behemoth he had hooked came to the surface and I can see it yet, an enormous silver body twisting and turning as it came near. Because the fish was too large to net, I slipped my hand into its crimson gills and with a great heave dropped it into the canoe. It was a trout three feet long and about seven inches wide and must have weighed thirty pounds or more. Back at camp we cut off huge steaks and broiled them over the fire because they were far too big for the frying pan. Served with tea and bannock, that trout was a feast.

There are many kinds of waiting in this world, such as looking forward to fall foliage color. One begins to notice the change in August, and in the far northern tundras a full month before that. One is thrilled at the slightest show, watching every increase day by day until at last the whole country bursts into shades of fire red, yellow, and orange.

It is the same in the spring when watching for the aspen on the ridges to turn green and the birches a rosy hue, a sign spring is here. Trees are not the only indication, however, for marsh marigolds become bright gold in the swamps, pussy willow

OF TIME AND PLACE

catkins take on a tint all their own, and against the snowbanks the red osier dogwoods show up red. All have blushed the countryside with the beauty of early spring.

One of the most exciting things when trout fishing is to wait for the first mayfly hatch, which brings the trout to the surface after a long winter of feeding on caddis worms and other larvae on the bottom. This is the signal for all fishermen to move on to the important business of catching brookies.

Waiting has a deep psychological impact on all of us and most people know it is not necessarily the waste of time it might appear to be at the moment. Waiting gives us a chance to realize we cannot solve the complicated puzzles of our lives without considering the vast complex series of variables that have a bearing on everything we do.

The Shining
Big Sea Water

Lake Superior has dominated my dreams since the days of my boyhood. Its beauty has power over those living near, and for the Indians especially the lake has great religious significance as the dwelling place of their sacred Manitou, who lives in its azure depths.

As a boy and a young man, I lived on Chequamegon Bay, on the south shore of Lake Superior, from which I could see the Apostle Islands; Madeline Island, the largest of all, was one of the early Indian settlements and headquarters of the fur trade, the site of countless battles and raids between invading Indian tribes and Indians and white men. Radisson and De Groseilliers spent a winter nearby during the 1660's when they explored the country beyond the north shore for the first time.

I was restless and dreamed of some day crossing the lake to the north shore, where I could explore the wild country of lakes, rivers, and forests that eventually became my home and where I have spent most of my life. When I finally made the crossing and headed inland, those first adventures in the Quetico-Superior country opened the door to the vast land of the Northwest Territories and the tundra as far as the Arctic Ocean. My travels took me everywhere—the Yukon, Alaska, and the shores of Hudson Bay.

The inland sea has meant much to me, as have the countless rivers with their cascades that plunge into it. The sea gulls and terns still wheel and swoop, and ducks swim in the surf as you travel the highway along its shore. Though things have changed since I knew it, the lake is still pristine and primitive, and I have not forgotten those early adventures or those of later years.

The country known as the Stony is a small part of the grand legacy of rivers, creeks, and lakes that flow into Lake Superior. In my early days the area was important to me, and I was very familiar with it. The Stony country lies in the great Laurentian Divide, whose waters run north and west to Lake of the Woods, to the wild regions of upper Canada, and south to the Atlantic. It boggles the mind to even try to comprehend this tremendous sweep of terrain.

While I knew what the grand watershed of the Stony country meant, I often forgot it in the multitude of little adventures. Traveling south from Ely along the highway to Superior sixty miles from my home, I usually stop for a short while to remember what it had meant to me and to my comrades, most of whom are now gone. I see them all and think of the hunting we did together, the brook trout fishing in dozens of clear-water streams such as the Isabella, the Baptism, and the Manitou, flicking a fly over some pool alive with brookies at dusk. I can hear the lonely call of whitethroats and hermit thrushes and the chuckle of water in little rapids.

I often stand at the Sand River, where the waters of the

Stoney River pour through a narrow gap toward the east. I try to picture the way it looked before the road came through, when the marshes above and below were full of rice with ducks feeding everywhere, and can almost hear the whisper of their wings.

I also think of the time when my deer-hunting partner Dean Julius Santo came over the river carrying a deer, with the ice not more than a couple of inches thick, barely strong enough to hold a man's weight. It was dusk and I watched with apprehension and dismay—crunch-crunch-crunch, the ice cracking and groaning with each step he took. If he broke through he would be gone before I could reach him in that frigid water. I thought of starting out with a long pole, but the ice would not hold the two of us, and with him crossing a quarter of a mile away, there was not time.

When he finally came ashore I asked him why he had taken such a terrible chance. "I shot this doe," he said, "and rather than drag it through the woods at night, I thought it would be easier to take it across the ice."

Another time not far from where Santo crossed the river, another hunter shot at me, no doubt thinking I was a deer. I happened to be on a snowy hillside with little cover, and across the valley were dense woods. I heard the spat-spat-spat of rifle fire and bullets hitting the ground very close, and I could see the red flash of his gun. I threw myself to the ground, firing my own gun as a warning. Another fusillade and then silence. The man must have realized his error and left.

In that same area one of our companions was lost; when he did not return to camp we were afraid he might have fallen. We searched for him all afternoon and during the night. In the morning I was the first to see him. He was running, and the more I called, the faster he ran. When I finally caught up to him I brought him down in the snow. In his panic and utter exhaustion he had run in circles most of the time, never stopping to rest, nor did he think of firing three shots, always the distress signal in deer country. Shamefacedly he returned to camp, saying nothing about the worry and trouble he had caused, and the rest of us tried to forget it.

All such recollections are merely personal footnotes to the grand story of Lake Superior. To me and many it is a land of treasured memories, some of grief and sadness, others of joy and happiness. No matter how trivial, we knew the Manitou spirit who dwells in the deeps would understand and evaluate their importance.

The mighty waves will still crash against the cliffs and beaches, and purple vistas never fade, though centuries pass and those who have known them are gone like the morning mists which disappear before the sun.

Let Superior speak for itself, telling its own story of the past, present, and future. Though changes have come, it is still part of the old wilderness and the Mother of Waters still sings her ancient song.

The Islands

I have always wanted to write about islands; they are different
from other places and give one a feeling of isolation from the
rest of the world. Because of their distance from the mainland,
all forms of life on an island develop in strange and wonderful
ways. Darwin, during the voyage of the *Beagle,* stopped at
many Pacific islands and found exotic species never seen before. His impressive discoveries were noted in a book, *On the
Origin of Species,* which changed man's concept of evolution
—not only of the creatures Darwin had found, but of man
himself.

I do not intend to describe faraway places, only the islands
I know intimately in the Quetico-Superior country and the
Northwest Territories of Canada. Most are little islands scattered everywhere, but to me they are as exciting in their own
particular way as those Darwin found.

The Hayes River on the way to the western coast of
Hudson Bay has an island over which I portaged one day

when the rocks were slippery and treacherous. Just before I reached the end, on a smooth glistening ledge covered with sleet my feet went out from under me and I fell face down, injuring myself quite severely, an unpleasant memory to say the least.

There is an Arctic island in the far reaches of this country on the way to Great Bear Lake. Just before we reached this large lake I was drawn by the silhouette of a barren spit of rock not more than a hundred yards long. Over its crest were grasses and brilliant orange lichens so characteristic of this area, brightened by the cold Arctic sun. When I look at a color shot of this sight, I feel it represents all of that wild barren expanse of the tundra and land of little trees.

Pine Island on Burntside Lake, not more than a mile west of my cabin, has the last large growth of virgin pine in the area. The huge trees are over three hundred years of age, and whenever I am beneath them I think of how young those pines were when the first explorers came through in 1660. When one listens to the nuthatches in the high tops one realizes this is the way all islands in the lake looked until the loggers came in about 1900. How that stand escaped is a mystery; the owner must have held the lumberjacks off with a .30-.30 rifle to save his trees from the fate of the rest.

Glacier Island is a smooth rock not far from the old pines set aside by the Nature Conservancy a few years ago as a wilderness; less than two hundred feet long and fifty wide, it is small but beautiful. Because of the southwest gales that sweep this part of the lake, the scraggly little pines all point the way of the wind. One of my old voyageur friends, Tony Lovink of Ottawa, a companion of many canoe trips in the Far North, loves this island, and it is always a joy to be there with him when he visits here.

Close to Pine Island is another small one like Glacier. There is a fine shelf of rock for landing a canoe, and each time I stop there I say it is as pretty a campsite as any in the Quetico.

Shortiss Island, larger than the other islands I have mentioned, is found in Lac la Croix on the U.S.–Canadian border. A cliff just across from our overnight camp has some of the finest pictographs in the region. There are the usual paintings of moose, pelicans, and strange horned monsters of the deep, but also hand pictographs the Indians painted on the rock as a special tribute to a great hunter. I often wonder why; perhaps it was a reward to a great warrior for the role he had played in some expedition. To allow him to dip his hands in the brownish ocher they used may have been a coveted mark of distinction. Not far away is Warriors' Hill, where young men raced each other over the smooth steep hill to show their strength and prowess to the elders. Legends and spiritual beliefs are part of this island.

Brent Island is on a lake with a broad sweep of water to the north. From here you can watch the northern lights playing and dancing in all colors across the black horizon. As a bonus, on the reefs around are some of the finest walleye pike one could wish to catch, and just by casting from the shore. There are bass and northern pike in the swampy bays that tempt one to stay there forever rather than travel on to other lakes.

Haystack Rock on the North Kawishiwi River is a small pyramidal rock formation, too tiny for a campsite, but it plays a part in the ecology of the region. At one time a sea gull had its nest near the base and loons may have nested there too. A family of beaver built their house nearby and moose wade in to feed on lily-pad roots. There are mink and otter as well as blue herons and ducks eating the wild rice. From this small vantage point one can see most of the wildlife of the area. Size is no measure of importance.

Fall Lake has a small island at the entrance to a rice-filled river leading to the east and connecting with a series of tiny ponds. Years ago when duck hunting was a passion with me, I spent many happy hours there; I never camped, only built a blind of brush and cattails to screen us from our spread of decoys. It was an exhilarating place; the mallards came in to start the season, and then toward its end there were bluebills and butterballs.

The Saganogons River on the Canadian side of the border has a strange island, for there is a rough portage with a tiny ledge just big enough for a tent about halfway to its end. The river foams and plunges on both sides, and when it is dark one wonders what would happen if one stumbled and plunged into the boiling rapids. The river runs violently on toward Kawnipi, a large lake to the north and a favorite route to many other waterways. Elizabeth and I camped there one stormy night and feasted on walleye pike and biscuits baked in a reflector oven. We have often spoken of that evening on the river, because of all islands this for us is the most exciting.

These are some of the islands I have known, each with a character of its own, and no doubt I could find hundreds more if I searched my memories. Islands will always intrigue me, and whenever I am on a canoe trip it is my hope at the end of the day to find one to camp on, a continent of my own.

A Point in Time

When I was a young guide in the Quetico-Superior country, I liked to roam on my own. Once I asked Dusty Rhodes, a daredevil bush pilot, to drop me at a lake and pick me up at a designated spot later. We took off on a bright sunny morning and headed north. After half an hour of flying, I pointed out a tiny spruce-bordered pond. Dusty looked it over, made several passes, and then glided in.

"This place will be hard to get out of," grumbled Dusty. "I shouldn't have come in the first place."

After he had untied the canoe from the pontoon and thrown out my packs, he started the motor and headed toward the center of the pond, but each time he had to drop back. "Those blasted spruce," he said, "are just too tall and I can't seem to clear them." He tried several more times with the same result.

"Wait a minute." he said, "I've got an idea. It just might work."

He rummaged around in the back of the plane and came out

with a coil of manilla rope, a stout three-quarter-inch hawser.

"Look," he told me, "I'll tie one end to the plane, the other to this big stump beside us. I'll climb in, rev up the motor until it's just bouncing on the water. Then you take your ax, and when it seems the motor can't roar any louder or the plane bounce any higher, really straining at the leash, you can cut the rope with one swift slash."

He climbed into the cockpit, and when the proper time came I cut the rope. The plane took off almost vertically and in nothing flat cleared the spruce. I stood there laughing with relief, listening to the drone in the distance to the south, and after it was gone I gathered my outfit together, pulled the canoe back of the stump, and pitched my camp. I was glad we had designated another pick-up spot.

Timing is an essential element in running a rapids on the Basswood River. At the head of the rapids—just above Wheelbarrow Portage—is a smooth rock against which the current caroms as a billiard ball bounces off the banking edge of the table. Coming down one must make the approach exactly right. I know that a number of canoes have smashed against that rock, the powerful water twisting and breaking them until there was nothing left to recognize. What happened to the occupants was anyone's guess, but I know there were drownings there. Once a man tried to come upstream in a canoe with a small outboard motor. He never arrived. I was a member of a crew that went looking for his body; we spent a week searching in the whirlpool just below. Finally in desperation we strung a net across the river, positive he would be found there, and we were right. It was a sight one tries to forget.

Voyageurs during the fur trading days of a couple of centuries ago often hit that rock amidships with their great birchbark canoes, spilling the precious contents of trade goods into the water, while the men who never learned to swim scrambled for the nearby shore. Many did not make it, according to diaries and records of the explorers. No wonder such accidents happened on the river, for there were trading posts on Basswood Lake which supplied the men with high wine or rum as a last regale before leaving for the hinterlands of the Northwest. The timing of those happy and carefree voyageurs was a little off, resulting in tragedies. I have had the good fortune to participate in scuba diving operations at this place and others and can vouch for the authenticity of the records; axes, kettles, muskets, flint, steel, and other artifacts have been recovered there.

In my cabin on Burntside Lake hangs a magnificent rack of horns, the most beautiful and symmetrical I have ever seen, from a huge buck I shot long ago in the Stony River country. I was hunting alone in a rugged country north of the river and had worked my way through a number of glacial potholes and high ridges. I often climbed to the crest to study a boggy heather below, on the chance a deer might be feeding there.

Lying in such a spot that day, I thought I saw something move but was not sure, and then I knew it was a big buck standing in the very center. The vegetation was so high the animal at times was hidden from view. It was a long way off, too far for a shot—one would have to be plain lucky at best —so I studied the situation and wondered if I should take a chance. I might wound the deer or miss it entirely, and there was the wind to consider and the fact that my quarry was downhill from me, a difficult problem of logistics. Finally I decided to try. I raised my sights as far as possible but knew this meant nothing at such long range. I would have to hold the rifle higher instead and just guess at the proper slant. I considered all this, stopped breathing, and fired.

At the report the buck disappeared. I ran down the hill but could see nothing; I sat on a hummock of grass thinking the animal might jump to its feet if grazed. Then to my amazement I saw the tip of a horn, a golden tip, but there was no movement—the buck was dead. I went over to where it lay and saw the bullet hole through the spine; the impact must have dropped him instantly. Then I saw the beautiful rack of horns. After dressing out the animal I cut off the horns with my hand ax, placed them on top of the first load of venison, and climbed back up to the ridge. The distance, when I paced it off on my return, was four hundred yards—an impossible achievement for me, but everything had simply worked together.

Though brook-trout fishing may seem a long departure from Dusty Rhodes, Wheelbarrow Rapids, and the shooting of the big buck on the Stony, all have something in common. When you stand in a pool, see the trout rising, and wonder why they ignore the tantalizing artificial flies you flutter across the edge, you realize they know something about timing too: that there is a direct correlation between their movement and whether your creel will be heavy or light.

All these are points in time, man taking a chance by doing something different, skating close to the razor's edge, having the curiosity and inventive genius to do something about things—the difference between man and the animal kingdom. We should be proud, and humble, for what we have done.

Falling Waters

Places of mystery have always intrigued us, with their power to trigger memories of hosts of happenings in the past. Elizabeth and I stayed on an island on Crooked Lake one mysterious moonlit night, and our intuition told us it would be one to remember.

Our tent was pitched on a secluded island at the entrance of Moose Bay on a small point a few miles below Basswood Falls. We had often stopped here on our way north to Robinson Lake or west to Lac la Croix. From here we could see the moon overhead, but we longed for the sight of the plunging waters of the Basswood River as they churned their boisterous way over three falls into the upper bay of Crooked Lake. At the bottom of Basswood River the foam-laced waters were all around us and we were thrilled and breathless, but the effort was worthwhile, for that upper bay of the lake was full of mist and thunder. It seemed we could actually hear the songs of the voyageurs as they came through on the portage—the thumping of their packs on the bare rocks of the landing and their shouts as they loaded their canoes on the way to the far Northwest. If there was moonlight when the voyageur brigade came by, its members, too, must have been excited by the charm of the scene before them. Knowing voyageurs as I did, I felt they could not help but respond.

We spent an hour watching the miracle of brilliant shifting lights and changing patterns on the swirling waters. Then because it was late, we paddled the three miles of moonlit water, past the Picture Rocks glowing in the light, and soon were among the dark brooding pines of our campsite on the island. The moon was still bright, and we could hear the roar of the falls in the distance.

Another time I was alone in the valley of Yosemite, and because it was early spring the falls plunging off the cliffs cascaded down as silver plumes of light. I thought of the gorgeous falls of Yellowstone northeast of Yosemite, the place the National Park Service had always called "one of the crown jewels of the system." One day below the great yellow canyon with its tremendous roar I understood why everyone who had seen it felt the same way. It was very beautiful, a picture postcard where people from all over the world came to stand in awe and wonder. Few came back to watch it in the moonlight, for it was dangerous in the dark on the loose crumbling formation and the climb down the narrow trail to the lookout was treacherous.

I like to remember Niagara Falls plunging over its great escarpment to a giant whirlpool far below. I saw it once with colored lights and was appalled at the embellishment. It is the same with Chatterton Falls in the Quetico, Curtain Falls at the outlet of Crooked Lake, and Silver Falls below Cache Bay of Saganaga. Such places need no colored lights; they are perfect

as they are and have the same impact on everyone. Partridge Falls beyond the wild rapids of Pigeon River and after the long portage from Grand Portage Post on Lake Superior to Fort Charlotte at the other end casts its own particular spell. To an early traveler, exhausted after the desperate toll of the long carry, sitting there at dusk just at the brink of the falls with the moon lighting the water, it would seem unreal as the mists boiled up from an unseen canyon hundreds of feet below. He would be filled with terror of the unknown and the dark wilderness he was about to enter.

In the Northwest Territories of Canada I remember Eagle Falls in the moonlight, with large trout boiling up over the surface of the pool below. We had come up the Camsell route over the tundra and taiga and were on our way to Great Bear Lake and the Mackenzie. It was bitterly cold when we made the portage around the falls and stood at its other end. This time, however, we were not intrigued; all we wanted was a good campsite, warm food, and a solution for the racing waters below us. The thrill was gone, for we faced stark reality.

Falling waters in the moonlight are unforgettable. They fill one with a strange subconscious feeling of both dread and delight.

Sacred Land

Not long ago I flew across the Quetico-Superior country to attend the funeral of an old friend and co-worker, Charley Erickson, who loved the wilderness and fought for years to preserve its haunting beauty. Charley looked like a Viking with a red beard and piercing blue eyes. When I first saw him it was like meeting a son of Eric the Red, one of the first to explore and colonize the North American continent. He was more than a Viking, however; he was a voyageur at heart and felt about the lake country he had chosen for his home as the voyageurs did when they landed in the far Northeast. He also loved this wild and unsettled country's freedom to roam.

Charley lived on an island of Nym Lake, north of Quetico Provincial Park, and spent the last years of his life teaching children the secret of his own love and awareness of the land. To transport young guests from his lodge on the mainland to the island, he had a thirty-five-foot Montreal canoe, the type the voyageurs of old used in traveling from Montreal on the

St. Lawrence down the Great Lakes on their way to the Northwest in search of fur and the route to China and the Orient.

The day I flew across the vast area to Nym was a cold and stormy one, with flurries of snow and sleet in the air. It was November and the kind of day Charley would have chosen for his departure. His casket was a simple one of pine, and his grieving friends had laid a swath of pine boughs on it and strapped it in the center of one of the big Montreals for the voyage home.

Following the funeral canoe was a second Montreal, paddled by his young friends. As they struggled in the teeth of a bitter wind, they sang the old French chansons of the voyageurs; it was good to hear their voices in unison to the tempo of their strokes. Arriving at the landing dock, they carried the casket reverently to a simple outdoor chapel under the pines. A few words of tribute, a prayer, and a final song, and it was over. Charley's ashes were later strewn over the wilderness lake country he cherished. To me that chapel will forever be a sacred place. Even with the drifting snow it was meaningful, for Charley was at home in all weather. He rests now in the lakes, rivers, and vistas of the land he loved.

There are many sacred places I have written of in the past —those that have more than ordinary meaning and where Indians never spoke for fear of disturbing the spirits. No Place Between, on the Kawishiwi, is such a place. The pictographs on Darkey, Crooked, and La Croix speak of the spirit world and for centuries were part of the poetry and religious ritual. Music and dance, the Valhalla of the Vikings, the ghost dance of the Indians, all represent the eternal striving of mankind for expression in the search for meaning. Charley was now with the Vikings, his funeral an essential element of what he had known, the deeper hidden world that spoke of mystery and the unknown.

One of my treasures is a voyageur's chapeau given to me by Charley's son. I look at it with reverence. It is bright red, woven of wool as the hats were long ago, and speaks of the days when brigades of red-capped voyageurs paddled down the lakes. It was the color of the wilderness, one that stood out against the dark brooding pines and brought out life and spirit. I can see those paddles tipped with red and the crimson paintings on the bows and sterns of the big canoes.

That hue was also the color of combat. Just before his passing Charley had met with members of the government, pleading with them to halt a hydro project that would have brought an acid rain over the Quetico and the Boundary Waters on the United States side of the border, destroying mosses and lichens as well as the great conifers of the area and all forms of life that lived in the shallow topsoil covering the glaciated Precambrian shield. Before this effort he had been instrumental in getting the Ontario government to halt a great logging project which would have crisscrossed the territory with all-weather roads, destroying every semblance of the wilderness he cherished.

Now this is over for Charley, but what he did will be remembered. His life is symbolic of the vital importance of fighting for the preservation of places sacred to him and to many. The thousands who will come to the lake country will learn why he fought so gallantly to preserve it.

Let's drink a toast to a man and a Viking who is now in the Valhalla of his ancestors.

The Music
of Spring

The winter had been long and hard, an endless series of difficult months. The squawk of the ravens cruising over the whiteness looking for food had been melancholy. Only the chickadees and bluejays stayed, and even they seemed to be halfhearted in their calling. The beautiful red and gray pine grosbeaks appeared only occasionally, then drifted off to warmer climes.

No wonder as February and March came we longed for the sun and warmth of spring, some variation to the doleful music; but still the cold dragged on and it seemed there would never be any change. How often I had said, "With the winds of March, spring cannot be far behind."

With April things finally began to happen. One morning as the sun rose I thought I heard the delightful trill of a purple finch and listened carefully to be sure. Each year several pairs had nested on the hill, an omen of the future. Later that day I heard a white-throated sparrow, "Oh Canada-Canada-Canada." It reminded me of their plaintive notes often drifting down at dusk while I stood in the water casting a rise for trout.

Now the chickadees were singing their mating call, and spring appeared to be here and the long wait over. One evening I heard a woodcock, saw it climb into the sky and then plunge back to earth making a strange exciting whistle as the air raced through the primary feathers. I had watched this mating ritual many times over the years. It reminded me that the mud flats in the swamp were soft and full of food and the nesting would soon be under way.

At my cabin on Listening Point there was still plenty of ice, but there were open leads along the shore and the sea gulls had come in to stake out their claims to a rookery. Like the woodcocks returning to their swamp, the gulls always flocked to the same place—a rock out in the open water or an island where during the summer they would bombard any canoe that approached the gray, clumsy chicks. How could they remember where to go with the millions of lakes on the way north?

Early one morning I watched a loon flying over from a lake just south to its old nesting site, which was near where the gulls nested. There was always a squabble about who had territorial rights of possession. A few days later as the ice blackened and the leads widened I saw a pair below the cabin. They were unafraid and, when I got close, simply dove and then reappeared a short distance away. The following days we heard their wild, rollicking laughter and that of others far out on the lake. One call was like that of a wolf, with a note of sadness in it. The great Finnish composer Sibelius used it for his theme in the classic *Finlandia*. The Canada geese were returning too; undulating arrows of flight patterns were etched against the sky, accompanied by a wild clamor as they flew toward nesting grounds far up into the Arctic.

The red-winged blackbirds soon drifted in, the males re-

splendent in red epaulets, and when they rose as a flock there was a startling flash of color. I could hear them in the swamps clinging to a reed or willow bush, conkoree-conkoree-conkoree. Three snow geese came in to feed and rest on the Burntside River; much whiter than the Canada with black wingtips, they would follow them into the Arctic tundras.

Tree swallows had been around for some time investigating the birdhouses for bluebirds and martins. Metallic blue in the back, white underneath, they added a special note of beauty and grace to the entire spring pageant.

The sight that really brought the old feeling of spring was to see the killdeer, with their long high killdee-killdee song, flying over any area that had open water, darting in with a streak of white, only to take off if disturbed and then return. It was good to hear a partridge drumming. All I could think of was a fallen log, and the cock in full color, ruff extended, strutting along to the end, then beating its wings rapidly against its chest, building up to a crescendo until the air was full of thunder—boom-boom-boom. After a while it would repeat the ritual to the other end of the log, telling some female he was truly cock of the walk.

There were two latecomers still to be heard from, a pair of orioles and the robins. Each year an orchard oriole nested in the tall birches south of the house, building a hanging nest in a secluded place. I knew they liked oranges so I fastened some in the crotches of trees and hung strands of fiber from a hemp rope they could pick up and use. Once in a great while I'd hear the peter-peter-peter high in the trees, but we seldom had even a glimpse of the orange and black beauty darting through the tops.

It was amusing to watch the robins when they came north, hopping around, hopefully listening for elusive angleworms that as yet had not been drawn to the surface by the warmth. They knew, however, that the rains would soon come and their troubles be over. Each morning they would herald the dawn with liquid music.

And finally, I heard the frog chorus in the swamp, the old primeval chorus that had echoed in the swamps of the carboniferous era millions of years ago. This song of the diminutive leopard frog, descended from the great ones, was as musical as that of the birds. I listened to my modern friends with delight, for they had sealed the doom of winter with the mighty sound of a thousand voices.

An Ethic
for the Land

A land ethic is a philosophical point of view involved with morality and character. One is not born with a feeling for ethics and the land, nor can a child comprehend its meaning though sensitive to what he sees and absorbs of the world of nature. A youth seldom has it, but as he matures into manhood he begins to grasp a vague sense of oneness and belonging. In old age he gains perspective and wisdom and can look back into the past and forward into the future.

All the places I have written about are part of the total picture of the earth and how we feel toward it. We ask ourselves if we are doing what is right. Are we good stewards? Have we done all we could to stop ugliness, devastation, and decay in the world around us? If the answer is yes, then we have embraced what is meant by a land ethic.

I question if I have done nothing that might change the character of islands where I have camped, if I have left them as pristine and unspoiled as when I arrived, and my campsite immaculately clean with kindling and firewood waiting for the next visitor. An affirmative reply gives me a warm feeling.

Lakes pose an entirely different problem from islands. It seems anything you might do to their vast waters would never be noticed. The whole idea of ethics seems relatively unimportant in such a setting. Does it really matter if you clean your fish on the smooth glaciated ledges beside the water, leaving the rotted, maggoty remains to offend others? It may seem utterly silly not to use detergent in your dishwater. But all such practices have an impact on the purity of the water. It is the cumulative habits of many which determine what happens to the environment. You may feel that whatever you do will never be noticed, for the waves will wash your sins away leaving no signs of anyone having been there. You may now have just a slight growing consciousness of guilt about your behavior, a sign perhaps of growing maturity.

Some of the rivers I have traveled all over the North have been drastically altered by the impact of man. Dams have been built across them, eliminating historic portages and making huge flowages look like a succession of beaver ponds with trees once green and growing now dead and ugly above the flood. The entire ecology of the area has been destroyed and the habitats of all living things changed.

In our search for energy we have often done such things to a river because almost everyone is strongly in favor of the projects due to their impact on the economy and employment. They ask why all the potential waterpower should go to waste. Who cares if a sparkling rapids is destroyed or the thunder of a plunging waterfall is stilled forever? Are not jobs more important than free and wild flowing rivers? And who remembers Indians and voyageurs except a handful of old historians and archeologists?

I think of what has happened to the mighty Churchill River, the major route of exploration and trade in the Northwest for over three centuries. Its history alone should have been reason enough to save it. It was the ancestral hunting and fishing grounds of the Indians. However, the construction of great multiple dams across it has resulted in lakes that have flooded those grounds, forcing the Indians to change their ancient way of life.

There are areas in the Far North, the Yukon and Kuskokwim deltas of southeastern Alaska, where millions of swans, geese, and ducks thrill us with the sound of their music and fill us with strange primeval excitement when great undulating skeins of them soar over in the spring and fall. Our ancestors must have watched them too and wondered where they were going and why.

Wildlife refuges may not seem to have a relationship with rivers, but they do have much in common, for both need to be set aside to preserve their own identity. Man can do evil things to these seemingly impenetrable swampy regions; we also ditch the prairies, where wildfowl build their nests and breed, in the Midwest, in northwestern Canada, and in Alaska. All types of use have an impact but it is the effort of everyone that determines what takes place.

Those who hunt as well as those who simply revel at the sight of flocks against a sunset, the whisper of wings, or the booming roar of an unfettered rapids are being betrayed by the developers who care little about our heritage. What they want are greater stands of grain or more generators for waterpower. While these are vital in our attempt to feed the world or expand our energy resources, what developers do not realize is that there is no substitute for aesthetic values or an understanding of the true meaning of ethics.

Despite the battles to save this magnificent wilderness of lakes, rivers, and forests from air pollution, it is beginning to look as though this enormous effort has been in vain and the personal sacrifices of thousands over half a century or more are for naught.

Pollution comes from other sources too, from our own industrialized cities and from Europe, and really strikes home if it occurs close by though it is only part of the larger threat affecting everyone, all over the world. A land ethic means we must change our way of life if we are to combat it.

Ethical and moral questions and how we answer them may determine whether primeval scenes will continue to be a source of joy and comfort to future generations. The decisions are ours and we have to search our minds and souls for the right answers.

We must ask ourselves how we truly feel about what we have done to the planet during our brief tenure upon it. Are we really willing to do what we should, and are we mature enough to forget selfish interests? When critical areas are being threatened, will we stand up and fight for them no matter how unpopular such stands might be? Our most important goal is preservation of the land which is our home. We must be eternally vigilant and embrace the broad concept of an environmental ethic to survive.

Epilogue

I have written of many things and places, not all of mystery and beauty but with something in common, for they deal with a land of which we are an indelible part and of the wilderness from which we came.

No matter where I have roamed, a golden thread runs through it all, woven into the broad and colorful fabric of my life. It is my hope that others may discover what I have found in their search for the mother lode of their dreams.

The other evening as I watched the sunset, I began to think of what I had written in this new book. The sun went down as usual in the same identical notch in the hills across the bay. The flaming ball slowly sank into the black pinnacled horizon and then disappeared, leaving the sky a riot of color, the water an opalescent hue. A loon called as though to signal the end of the display before the coming of the dark.

I thought then of the cabin, the many voices there and the joy and laughter it had known; of my voyageurs down from

Canada, my Alaskan family visiting this summer, countless friends who had been there over the years. The cabin reverberated with the echoes of their voices. This was the place they loved to come at the time of their own choosing, a big part of our lives. There were many voices, from the high excitement and wonder of a child, through those of maturity, to the gentle sounds of old age. All these were part of what I have known and will never forget.

SIGURD F. OLSON (1899–1982) was one of the greatest environmentalists of the twentieth century. A conservation activist and popular writer, Olson introduced a generation of Americans to the importance of wilderness. He served as president of the Wilderness Society and the National Parks Association, and as a consultant to the federal government on wilderness preservation and ecological problems. He earned many honors, including the highest possible from the Sierra Club, National Wildlife Federation, and Izaak Walton League.

Olson's books include *The Singing Wilderness* (1956), *Listening Point* (1958), *The Lonely Land* (1961), *Runes of the North* (1963), *Open Horizons* (1969), *The Hidden Forest* (1969), *Wilderness Days* (1972), *Reflections from the North Country* (1976), and *Of Time and Place* (1982). His books created a new genre of nature writing that was infused with beauty and respect for our nation's wild places. He was a recipient of the John Burroughs Medal, the highest honor in nature writing, and his books frequently appeared on best-seller lists across the nation.

For most of his life, Olson lived and worked in Ely, Minnesota, gateway to the Quetico-Superior region.